Challenging Corporate Rule

The Petition to Revoke Unocal's Charter
as a Guide to Citizen Action

Challenging Corporate Rule

The Petition to Revoke Unocal's Charter as a Guide to Citizen Action

Robert Benson

THE APEX PRESS

Published by The Apex Press

Library of Congress Cataloging-in-Publication Data
has been applied for.

ISBN 1-891843-04-4

Printed on recycled, chlorine-free paper.

Printed in the United States of America

Contents

Dedicated to Paul Alan Smith

Foreword

by Ronnie Dugger*

This is a manual for citizen action to challenge corporate power. As you read it, know that you are not alone. You are invited to become part of a large movement of citizens who have realized at the same historical moment that we must reassert control over corporations, or else all is lost—our independence, our democracy.

I was among the speakers when a group of us presented to the attorney general of California our citizens' petition to revoke the charter of the Union Oil Company of California, at the Reagan Building in Los Angeles in September of 1998. Thinking of other citizens who may want to close miscreant corporations in other states, I said then that our purposes are even larger than they seem.

We are not seeking just the closure and reorganization of one oil company, though we need that. We are taking an important, open and public first step together, as citizens and citizen-organizations of the United States, to end the domination of our economics, our culture, our environment, our politics, our government, and our national life by large and irresponsible national and transnational corporations.

We are not just focusing here on one company's violations of laws to protect American citizens. We are saying that we, the people of the United States acting in our several states, chartered the U.S.-based transnational corporations that now range across the world—Unocal was chartered in California in 1890—and we assert our moral responsibility for, and there-

---

*Ronnie Dugger, former editor and publisher of the Texas Observer, author of biographies of Lyndon Johnson and Ronald Reagan, is co-chair of the Alliance for Democracy, one of the organizations petitioning the California attorney general to revoke the corporate charter of Unocal.

fore our democratic control over, offenses against people which our corporations commit or in which they become complicit anywhere and everywhere in the world.

We know that to take this position is "politically incorrect" at least in customary major-party politics. It's a no-no to admit, much less to assert, that we as citizens are incriminated by what our corporations do abroad. Democracy is not supposed to be to blame. But Americans are to blame, and democracy is to blame, and we here and now accept responsibility and start the long way back until the corporations we create are once again subordinate, in every way, to the will of the people.

Our forebears knew what they were doing, about corporations. For a hundred years our state legislators created corporations as agents of the democratic will, set the limits on what they could do, and closed them if they exceeded the authority the people gave them.

A hundred and twelve years ago, in 1886, the Supreme Court began the long process, which climaxed in the Bellotti case in the 1970s, of declaring in effect, in defiance of common sense and democracy, that corporations are people, and giving them the constitutional rights of people, including free speech. Since 1886 waves of corporate lawyers who put property over democracy have developed new theories of the corporation to defy democracy: the corporation, they pronounce, is only a private business association, a nexus of contracts that the people have nothing to do with—democracy has nothing to do with.

By giving our rights to what should have remained our subordinate creations, the judges of the Supreme Court, across time, have stolen our country from us. In consequence, the corporations are Supercitizens, and we are their subcitizens. The corporations are Superpersons, and we are their subpersons. And the corporations we created as servants of our public interest have broken free of our democratic control and metamorphosed into the international creatures of greed and rapacity that now dominate the world.

By this petition and our action together for it we are telling you that we the people have everything to do with you and that we are launching a broad citizens movement to make sure that you know it and remember it.

We the people have the right to control the shape and terms of our economic life, as well as our political life. What—God help us—we should have learned by now from the long history of civilization is that if the people don't control economic life, the inevitably gathering economic oligarchy, the plutocracy, will strangle democracy. That is what has been happening, again, in the United States since the defeat of the American populists at the end of the last century.

For the past 15 or 20 years now, the divine right of kings has been replaced by the divine right of CEOs and the controlling owners behind them. We are ruled now by a form of government in which hierarchical and authoritarian corporations control the government for their own profit and power against the people's interests.

President Franklin Roosevelt said in 1938, "The liberty of a democracy is not safe if the people tolerate the growth of private power to a point where it becomes stronger than their Democratic State itself. That, in its essence, is Fascism."

Look at us four decades later.

Regulation of the large corporations has been abandoned by the government. Antitrust laws are mounted in the trophy cases of the politicians. In 1997 we had 156 corporate mergers each worth more than a billion dollars. Big business fires workers for trying to form unions and gets away with it year after year. The corporate share of taxes has dropped in the last 50 years from 33% to 15% while the people's share of taxes has gone from 44% to 73%. One percent of the people among us own 40% of the national wealth. The savings and loan rake-off costs the taxpayers half a trillion dollars. The rate of child poverty among us is four times the rate in Western Europe. Forty million of us have no health insurance. The cigarette corporations go on killing for profit—who gives a damn? Sweatshops return to the garment industry. Who gives a damn! Huge conglomerate corporations control our newspapers and the broadcasts on our own public airways. Who gives a damn! Our jobs are exported to the low-wage areas of the world with no protections for the workers or environment abroad. Corporations not governments are 51 of the 100 largest economies in the world.

Four decades after that warning from Roosevelt, our elections are bought and we all know it. The government is no longer our government. It's these huge corporations' government and we all know it. As outgoing Senate Democratic Democratic Majority Leader George Mitchell of Maine said, "This system stinks. This system is money."

We speak out and act together now to hold the Union Oil Company of California accountable to the people, yes. But also to say with President Roosevelt that the huge national and transnational corporations have become more powerful than the democratic state itself. In this book you have in your hands the beginning of a new people's movement to take back our government from the corporations that have seized it and now abuse and misuse our democratic power, against democracy, around the world.

Introduction

By Robert Benson, Professor of Law
Loyola Law School, Los Angeles.
Lead attorney, National Lawyers Guild
charter revocation project.

I'm going to let you in on a little secret that big business doesn't want you to know: The citizens of every state, acting through their attorney general, have, and have always had, the legal authority to go to court to revoke the charters of corporations that violate the law. This means that lawbreaking corporations can be dissolved, put out of business, their assets sold to others under a judge's order that will protect jobs, the environment and the public interest.

In our democracy, corporations have no inherent right to exist. They exist by the permission of we the people acting through the legislature, the attorney general and the courts. Since we the people attach strings to the privilege of doing business in the corporate form (such as the condition that corporations actually obey the law!), when those conditions are violated we the people are perfectly free to yank those strings and pull the charters from offending companies.

Attorneys general used the legal tool of corporate charter revocation fairly frequently in the 19th century. In our own time, it has been less common but it remains on the books in every state and is occasionally invoked. In California, in 1976 the attorney general used it to force a private water company out of business for delivering contaminated water to its customers. The attorney general of New York state used this tool in 1998 in conjunction with other tobacco litigation to put the Council for Tobacco Research, a New York corporation, out of business and order its assets donated to state education and health institutions.

Most attorneys general, however, are letting this law enforcement device gather dust in their desk drawers. They don't even want you to know about it because the truth is they are soft on corporate crime and the corporate takeover of our democracy.

Attorneys general and big business want you to think that the cozy system of "government regulation" is working and nothing stronger is necessary. But the regulatory agencies that are supposed to keep corporations safe for the rest of us have been captured by the businesses they are assigned to oversee. The agencies are sucked into the quicksand of years-long efforts to protect the public one toxic spill at a time, one layoff at a time, one civil rights violation at a time. In the end, too often the corporations walk away with a light fine that they deduct from their taxes as a cost of doing business. And attorneys general get re-elected by deceptively boasting about the fines they imposed on polluters and other corporate criminals, never admitting that they could and should have put some of these incorrigible repeat offenders out of existence forever.

The book you have in your hand constitutes an effort to stir new life into the legal tool of corporate charter revocation. Emerging from a people's rebellion against corporate crime, it is a stone in David's slingshot cast against Goliath. We recalled that David toppled Goliath, so we did not shy from the struggle. National Lawyers Guild attorneys formed a broad coalition of environmental, human rights, women's, social justice and corporate democracy groups. We selected one giant corporate target—the Union Oil Company of California, or Unocal—that seemed to have violated a wider spectrum of laws in more places, over a longer period of time, and to have angered more people than most companies. Attorney Michelle Sypert and I researched allegations against Unocal and documented them in a long legal brief with nearly 400 footnotes. Then, in September of 1998, our legal team filed the whole thing with the attorney general of California, Unocal's home state, petitioning him to ask a court to dissolve the company. This book contains the complete petition.

Three business days after we petitioned the Republican attorney general, he responded with a terse rejection. He gave no explanation, but his letter noted a "cc" to the general counsel of Unocal. Clearly, the rejection was based on politics, not law. We could have sued the attorney general for abuse of discretion. A short time later, however, a new, Democratic attorney general was elected, so instead of suing we refiled the petition with the new office holder in April of 1999. He also declined to act. This disappointed but did not surprise us. We already knew that both political parties are in the pockets of corporate interests. As this book goes to press we are deliberating on whether to file suit or to continue gathering grassroots endorsements of our effort and refiling the petition until the light generated by the heat of populist anger helps the attorney general to see the law more clearly. This attorney general, Bill Lockyer, has said he wants to be known as a "Teddy Roosevelt," the great trust-buster. We will remind him that Teddy Roosevelt declared, "I am for men and not for property" and, "I rank dividends below human character." He did not cower, but stood up to the most powerful corporations of his day.

While we shall be unrelenting in our pursuit of Unocal for its egregious abuses, our goal has always been larger than victory over that single corporation. We aim to revive charter revocation across the country generally, to retrieve it from American history of the Populist era, to reinject it into our political discourse. We intend to educate the public about it, and to make attorneys general as comfortable with it as they are with any other law enforcement mechanism at their disposal.

Already, there is evidence that we are making significant headway toward these goals. Our petition has received extensive national and international attention in both the mainstream and business press. Reporters are intrigued to learn that corporate charters can be taken away. The idea that people can assert democratic control over corporate behemoths has struck a responsive chord in the public. Many citizens have written us and have phoned radio talk shows to tell us how relieved and optimistic they feel to learn the law is on their side against seemingly implacable corporate power. Our list of supporters has grown from the band of 30 original petitioning organizations and individuals to about 150 and counting, including some California state legislators, several mayors and city council members, clergy, scores of law professors from across the nation, and some of the most influential women's and environmental organizations in the nation. We have even moved Unocal a bit: *The New York Times* reports that our petition to revoke Unocal's charter was one of several pressures that led the company to abandon its negotiations with the anti-woman Taliban militia in Afghanistan.

We now present the petition in book form to help you and your organization deploy the charter revocation tool against other corporations in other struggles. We intentionally drafted the Unocal petition to be a model for this purpose. The petition:

• is written in plain English,

• describes the history and law of charter revocation,

• is organized to be used as a template for battles against other corporations with different facts,

• exhibits the depth and precision of documentation that is desirable in such a petition.

There is no one right way to do such a petition. Ours is one way. We invite others to improve upon it and to copy without attribution any parts of it that may be useful. No permission is needed. The petition is not copyrighted.

Here are some other key considerations as you draft your petition:

Remember, this is not a lawsuit. In most states, you are not filing a suit in court, but filing a document with your attorney general asking him or her to go to court on behalf of the public to revoke a corporation's charter. This gives rise to some confusion about what to call your document. We titled the Unocal document "Complaint Lodged with the Attorney General," because the California statute says the attorney general may take action "upon the complaint of a private party." But we decided to refer publicly to our document as the "Unocal Petition," because we are petitioning the attorney general to act. Unfortunately, the word "petition" suggests to many the sort of list of signatures you might gather on a clipboard in front of your supermarket on a Saturday morning. Our document, instead, is a lengthy legal brief.

Whatever it is called, the legal mechanism of filing a document with the attorney general is more attractive than a lawsuit because it avoids litigation costs and invokes the political process. On the other hand, if the attorney general turns you down, you then have to consider whether to sue to force action. If you decide not to sue, depending on the law of your state, you may continue to refile the document while conducting a media and grassroots campaign to pressure the attorney general to act favorably. In the final analysis, the charter revocation mechanism works through making elected officials politically accountable. There may already be litigation or other formal legal proceedings pending against the company. Charter revocation opens an additional front, offering a new way to attract support for your struggle.

A small corporation with a single, egregious violation may be as good a target as a mega-corporation with multiple offenses. We chose to pursue Unocal precisely because it represents the giant, multinational corporation with many different offenses over many years. As a result, our petition is lengthy and complex. But attorneys general may find it politically more feasible to put out of business a relatively small firm that has committed even a single horrendous act, such as intentionally emitting toxic chemicals over an elementary school. Your petition may be relatively short and simple. Pursuing small corporations before attacking a Fortune 500 company is a good way to build a solid record of recent precedents that will make it more difficult for an attorney general to ignore a demand for charter revocation of a large corporation. Of course, attorneys general cannot dissolve every company for every minor violation of law. They, and the courts, will always balance severity of the harm and impact on the public interest in making revocation decisions. The political and media perceptions of the contending sides will, inevitably, also come into play.

Be cautious in what you say about the target corporation. Although legal petitions to the government for redress of grievances may enjoy special free-speech protection, the corporation may think about suing you if you get your facts wrong. The rhetoric and deeply held beliefs of activist groups are poor guides for factual claims. Anchor facts in reliable sources. When possible, cite cases of legal violations that have been adjudicated and the target corporation found guilty. Be certain when you do to include the complete citation of the judgment.

Even then, it is best to state the facts as "allegations" in your petition. The petition need not prove facts itself. It is enough to state serious factual allegations that are sufficient to trigger a judicial hearing to prove the facts one way or the other. In developing the Unocal petition, we not only conducted a careful legal review for accuracy but also had the benefit of a line-by-line review by Ronnie Dugger, the author of the Foreword to this book and a life-long journalist, author and publisher. Try to obtain an independent review of this sort.

Research the company thoroughly. Here are some, among many, avenues of information. (1) Contact groups that have already sued the corporation. Ask them to share their research. Call their attorneys for their court documents. (2) Look for newspaper and trade magazine stories about the company in a computer data-base such as Lexis-Nexis. (3) Get records of reports and violations from state and federal regulatory agencies. Records from the federal Securities and Exchange Commission, Environmental Protection Agency, and Occupational Safety and Health Agency—as well as their state government counterparts—may be particularly useful. (4) Search a legal data-base such as Law Finder, Lexis-Nexis or Westlaw to turn up all reported judicial decisions involving the company. (5) Contact non-profit corporate research organizations that track corporate behavior. Multi-national Monitor in Washington, D.C., Transnational Resource and Action Center in San Francisco, and Data Center in Oakland, are three good ones. (6) Look at the corporation's own web site. Companies often post information that hoists them by their own petard.

Research as well the history of corporate law in your own state as we had to do it in California. Understand the different channels used in the past to assert democratic control over corporations, including legislative actions and judicial arenas. Define your short and long term goals as realistically as possible. Consider what combination of actions, including but not limited to charter revocation, are most likley to achieve these goals.

Know how jobs, environmental cleanup and tax revenues can be protected if the company is dissolved. You need to answer these questions in advance for labor, workers, environmentalists and government. Some groups may be suing the target corporation independently of your revocation action. It may well strengthen their position to support your efforts as a supplement to their lawsuits. They will want to know how their interests are protected in the event of dissolution. Have a lawyer check out your state's law, but in general, the answer to the question is that your petition will seek not only dissolution of the company but an immediate freeze of assets and appointment of a receiver under court supervision who will oversee sale of the assets in a manner that will preserve jobs, pay scales and union representation in any company assuming the assets; that will set aside guaranteed funds for environmental cleanup and any other liabilities; and that will order transfer of the assets to others who will remedy the harms for which the corporation has been dissolved. You may suggest to the attorney general and the court that an advisory committee be set up, consisting of the petitioners in your organization, labor, community and other interested groups, to guide the receiver's recommendations. Such groups could become the long-sought after mechanism by which corporations will be democratized.

Although you can do much of the work without a lawyer, legal review will be *indispensable*. Each state's legal requirements may differ. In several states, for example, citizens need not seek permission of their attorney general, but can file directly in court themselves. But beware of the trap in which you can find yourself if you take action on your own against a Fortune 500 company: you will be fighting an adversary with very deep pockets. In the case of our Unocal petition, we were in fact invited by the former California attorney general to ask his permission to proceed on our own, but we refused on the ground that only the state attorney general has the resources to fight a huge corporation. In every state, the precise statutory wording and case law of the charter revocation provisions must be studied. Our National Lawyers Guild team for the Unocal petition may be able to help locate an attorney in your state. We can be reached by e-mail at heed@igc.org. Environmental attorney Thomas Linzey of the Community Environmental Legal Defense Fund in Pennsylvania is a leading expert on charter revocation and may also be able to refer you to an attorney in your state. He can be reached by e-mail at tal@cvns.net

A media and grassroots campaign to raise public awareness and mobilize political support is as important as the petition itself. Some would say that such a campaign is even more important because without intense public pressure it is unlikely that the state attorney general will actually revoke the charter of a large corporation. The long-range goal is to get the public, media and politicians used to the idea that corporations are subordinate to the citizens who permit them to exist in our economy. So don't file your petition quietly by mail and wait for an answer from the attorney general. Use it as a tool to organize and inform like-minded interest groups, to educate the media, and to open a dialogue with politicians. We announced our Unocal petition at two well-attended simultaneous press conferences followed by press releases, printed a glossy brochure entitled "How Many Strikes Do Big Corporations Get?," then fielded speakers to community groups, and produced a 24-minute video. We asked our members to send "action alerts" to their mailing lists requesting that letters be sent to the attorney general. All the legal documents, press releases, brochure, updates, lists of endorsers, and ordering information for the video and for this book are available on our web-site: www.heed.net.

Keep your eye on other important charter revocation efforts. In Alabama, where citizens can apply to the courts directly to revoke corporate charters without going through their attorney general, state judge William Wynn acting as a private citizen has filed suit asking that five major tobacco companies have their privilege of doing business in that state wholly revoked. In New York State, where the last attorney general revoked the charter of the Council for Tobacco Research, the new attorney general,

Eliot Spitzer, campaigned on a platform of revoking corporate charters more frequently and has hired as his special counsel Carl Mayer, author of some of the most incisive legal scholarship on controlling corporate power. Attorney Thomas Linzey, mentioned above, regularly uses charter revocation petitions as part of his environmental practice and is not discouraged that he has yet to see his first victory. "In some states, reasserting democracy over corporate power will take a long-term struggle," Linzey says. "We're taking our inspiration from the early lawyers who mounted the battle against racial segregation and after many frustrating years ultimately prevailed. Charter revocation offers the opportunity to mobilize and open another front in the struggle."

If you know of other revocation actions, or if you hear that corporations are trying to amend your state statutes to foreclose the possibility of charter revocations, please contact us at heed@igc.org and we will help spread the word. Together, we will reestablish what the courts have always held: that corporations are "mere creatures of the state" and, in the words of U.S. Supreme Court Justice Byron White, "The state need not permit its own creation to consume it."

1 Cynthia Anderson-Barker, Working People's Law Center, Los Angeles (State Bar # 175764)
2 Professor Robert Benson, Loyola Law School (State Bar #68521)
3 José Luis Fuentes, Working People's Law Center, Los Angeles (State Bar #192236)
4 James Lafferty, Executive Director, National Lawyers Guild, Los Angeles
5
6 James Minuto (State Bar #106041)
Michelle Sypert (State Bar #181148)
7 For The International Law Project for Human, Economic & Environmental Defense (HEED), National Lawyers Guild, 8124 W. 3rd St, Suite 201, Los Angeles, CA 90048, Tel.: 213/736-1094. Fax: 213/380-3769. E-mail: heed@igc.org. Internet:www.heed.net
8
9

10

---

11 **COMPLAINT LODGED WITH THE ATTORNEY GENERAL OF CALIFORNIA**
12 **UNDER CALIFORNIA CODE OF CIVIL PROCEDURE § 803,**
CALIFORNIA CORPORATIONS CODE §1801
13

14 **TO REVOKE THE CORPORATE CHARTER**
OF
15 **THE UNION OIL COMPANY OF CALIFORNIA (UNOCAL)**
16 **by Petitioners**

17
• Action Resource Center
18 • Alliance for Democracy of U.S.A.
19 • Alliance for Democracy of Austin, Texas
• Alliance for Democracy of San Fernando Valley, California
20 • Gloria Allred, individual
21 • Amazon Watch
• Asian/Pacific Gays and Friends
22 • Burma Forum Los Angeles
• Democracy Unlimited of
23 Humboldt County, California
24 • Earth Island Institute
25 • Michael Feinstein, City Council Member,
Santa Monica, California, individual
26 • Feminist Majority Foundation
27 • Free Burma Coalition

28

HEED 8/98

1
2
3
4
5
6
7
8
9
10
11
12
13
14
15
16
17
18
19
20
21
22
23
24
25
26
27
28

• Free Burma — No Petro-dollars for SLORC
• Global Exchange
• Randall Hayes, individual
• National Lawyers Guild of U.S.A.
• National Lawyers Guild of Los Angeles, San Diego,
Santa Clara Valley and San Francisco
• National Organization for Women (NOW)
• National Organization for Women (NOW) of California
• Program on Corporations, Law and Democracy
• Project Maje
• Project Underground
• Rainforest Action Network
• Harvey Rosenfield, individual
• Surfers' Environmental Alliance
• Transnational Resource and Action Center

September 10, 1998

HEED 8/98

Contents

HEED 8/98

Table of Authorities

ADMINISTRATIVE AND LEGISLATIVE MATERIALS

HEED 8/98

CASES

HEED 8/98

HEED 8/98

HEED 8/98

INTERNATIONAL LAW

HEED 8/98

HEED 8/98

Commission on Human Rights on February 26, 1997,
1333rd session, 95th regular session.   116, 117

Slavery Convention (46 Stat. 2183, T.S. No. 788. 60
I.N.T.S. 253).   98

Stockholm Declaration (11 I.L.M. 1416), Rio Declaration
(31 I.L.M. 874).   71

U.N. Charter (59 Stat. 1031, 3 Bevans 1153 (1945))·

U.N. Convention on the Law of the Sea (21 I.L.M. 1261). 71

U.N. Economic and Social Council, Commission on
Human Rights, *1998 Situation of Human Rights in Myanmar*
(April 20, 1998).   101, 108, 111

U.N. Framework Convention on Climate Change
(31 I.L.M. 849).   71, 77

U.N. Human Rights Commission, March 17, 1993,
Burma News, April 1993, No. 4, Vol. 4, p. 4, available
on the University of North Carolina Internet site located
at ftp://sunsite.unc.edu/pub/academic/political-science/
freeburma/ba/.   96

U.N. Human Rights Commission, Draft Declaration on
the Rights of Indigenous Peoples,
E/CN.4/SUB.2/1994/2/Add.1 (1994).   116, 117

U.N. Human Rights Committee, *Communication No. 167/1984
Bernard Ominayak, Chief of the Lubicon Lake Band v. Canada,* 45th
Session, Supplement No. 40 (A45/40), Volume II, pages 1-30.   118

U.N. Human Rights Committee, No. 511/1992
Oct. 26, 1992. (Finland Herdsmen's case).   119

U.N. Human Rights Committee, Article 27:
8/4/94 General Comment 23.   118

LEGAL SCHOLARSHIP

(1996). 71

Thomas Linzey, "Awakening a Sleeping Giant: Creating a Quasi-Private Cause of Action for Revoking Corporate Charters in Response to Environmental Violations," 13 *Pace Environmental Law Review* 219 (1995). 41, 52

Thomas Linzey, "Killing Goliath: Defending Our Sovereignty and Environmental Sustainability Through Corporate Charter Revocation in Pennsylvania and Delaware," 6 *Dickinson Journal of Environmental Law & Policy* 31 (1997). 41

Carl J. Mayer, "Personalizing the Impersonal: Corporations and the Bill of Rights," 41 *Hastings L.J.* 577 (1990). 45

Arthur Miller, *The Supreme Court and American Capitalism* 15 (1968). 46

William L. Prosser, *Law of Torts* §46 (4th ed., 1971). 99

Robert Stumberg, *The New Supremacy of Trade: NAFTA Rewrites the Status of States* (Center for Policy Alternatives, Washington, D.C., September, 1993). 45

Janusz Symonides, "The Human Right to a Clean, Balanced and Protected Environment," 20 *International Journal of Legal Information* 24 (1992). 77

2 Witkin, *Summary of California Law: Agency and Employment* §135. 99

5 Witkin, *Summary of California Law: Torts* § 37 (9th ed., 1988). 99

NEWSPAPERS AND NEWS SERVICES (By Date)

New York Times , February 6, 1969 at 19 (New York

1	Times Information Bank Abstracts).	72
2 3 4	Greg Hartman, "ACWD Reaches Settlement in Water Fight with Citizens," *The Argus* (Fremont, California), March 26, 1976 at 1.	61
5	*The Nation*, Bangkok, June 23, 1993	101
6 7 8 9	*Bangkok Post Weekly Review*, May 13, 1994, available in Burma News, May 1994, No. 5, Vol. 5, p. 3, available on the University of North Carolina Internet site ftp://sunsite.unc.edu/pub/academic/political-science/ freeburma/ba/.	112
10 11 12	Jack Doyle, "Oil Slick: Profits Abroad and Poison at Home; Big Petroleum Ships Out, Leaving Behind a Big Mess," *Washington Post,* July 31, 1994.	83
13 14	Kristina Markus, "Still Ringing in Their Ears," *Chicago Tribune*, August 3, 1994.	82
15 16 17	Jack Danylchuk, "Lubicon, Catholic Order Force Debate on Start-Up of Unocal Sour Gas Plant," *The Edmonton Journal,* March 26, 1995.	119
18 19 20	Sam Fletcher, "Unocal Logs 2 Indonesia Discoveries; Horizontal Well In Gulf Doubles Output," *The Oil Daily*, May 23, 1995.	119
21 22	"In an Exploited Forest, an Indian Tribe Canada Forgot," *The Orange County Register,* August 4, 1996.	119
23 24	*Asia Times*, "Why Unocal Ignores Myanmar Sanctions," August 13, 1996, at 9.	103
25 26	Interview with John F. Imle, President of Unocal, *Asia Times*, August 13, 1996.	114
27 28	"Taliban's Unlikely Story," *Moneyclips*, October 17, 1996 (Source: Al Ahram Weekly).	86

HEED 8/98

"Taliban = Death and Humiliation for Homosexuals," *The Observer* (London), February 23, 1997. 94

Nancy Rivera Brooks, "Union Says Tosco Threatened Closure," *Los Angeles Times*, March 26, 1997, at D-2. 82

"Unocal Guilty of Dumping a Chemical Into San Francisco Bay," *New York Times* , April 20, 1997, at I-23. 74

Reese Erlich, "Burma-Business: Oil Giant Suffers Legal Setbacks," *Inter Press Service*, May 8, 1997. 74

"EPA Fines Unocal For '94 Toxic Release," *San Francisco Chronicle*, May 9, 1997, at A23. 74

"CITGO Takeover of Uno-Ven Illinois Refinery Ruffles Workers," *Dow Jones Telerate Energy Service*, May 20, 1997. 81

James Gerstenzang, "Oil Executive Breaks With Industry," *Los Angeles Times*, May 21, 1997 at A-3. 77

David Johnson, "As CITGO Takes Over at Lemont, Labor Strife Looming," *Platt's Oilgram News,* May 23, 1997. 81

Michael Hytha, "Study Blames Illness on Unocal Leak," *San Francisco Chronicle* , August 21, 1997 at A17. 74

John D. Cox, "Once-Popular Avila Beach Goes From Tourists to Toxic," *Sacramento Bee*, September 8, 1997 at A1. 72, 74

Kenneth Freed, "Odd Partners in UNO's Afghan Project," *Omaha World-Herald,* October 26, 1997. 92

Maggie O'Kane, "A Holy Betrayal: The Taliban, Islam's Warriors, Have Launched Jihad Against Their Own Afghan Countrywomen," *The Guardian,* November 29, 1997. 86

Caroline Lees, "International: Oil Barons Court Taliban

1 in Texas," *The Sunday Telegraph London*, December 14, 1997. 90

2 Jean Dubail, "Global Warming; Best Scientific Minds Agree:
3 The Need To Act Is Clear," *Cleveland Plain Dealer*,
   December 15, 1997 at 9B.   77
4

5 Ed Vulliamy, "U.S. Women Fight Taliban Oil Deal," *The
6 Guardian Foreign Page*, January 12, 1998.   90

7 Hugh Pope, "Pipeline Dreams: How Two Firms' Fight for
8 Turkmenistan Gas Landed in Texas Court," *The Wall
   Street Journal*, January 19, 1998.   90
9

10 "US Oil Company Team Holds Talks with Taliban on
   Exploration Plan," *Agence France Presse*, February 14,
11 1998.   91

12

13 Martha M. Hamilton, "Global Warming Gets a 2nd
   Look; Oil Executives Are Shifting Their Stance," *The
14 Washington Post*, March 3, 1998 at C01.   77

15
   Danielle Knight, "Environment: U.S. Greens Join
16 Protest Against Thai Pipeline," *Inter Press Service*,
17 February 23,1998.   79

18 R. Jeffrey Smith, "Burma's Image Problem Is a
19 Moneymaker for U.S. Lobbyists," *The Washington Post*,
   February 24, 1998 at A-19.   126
20

21 "Surfers' Environmental Alliance," *City News Service*,
   Los Angeles, March 10, 1998.   72
22

23 Nancy Dunne, "Anger Over WTO Turtle Ruling,"
24 *Financial Times* (London, March 14, 1998) at 3.   46

25 Sayed Salhuddin, "Asia: Taliban Execute Two People
26 Convicted of Sodomy," *Reuters*, March 23, 1998.   94

27 Christopher S. Wren, "Road to Riches Starts In The
28 Golden Triangle," *New York Times*, May 11, 1998 at A-8. 127

HEED 8/98

1   Jack McCarthy, "Mine Company Sued Over Tainted
    Water," *The Press Enterprise*, May 20, 1998.   75
2

3   "Taliban Hope To Begin Building Afghan Pipeline by
    End of 1998," *Agence France Presse*, May 22, 1998.   91
4

5   "Afghan Factions Strike Deal To Build Gas Pipeline,"
    Itar-Tass, June 6, 1998.   91
6

7   Kenneth Freed & Jena Janovy, "UNO Partner Pulls Out
8   of Afghanistan Project," *Omaha World-Herald*, June 6,
    1998.   93
9

10   Dan Morgan and David B. Ottaway, "Women's Fury
     Toward Taliban Stalls Pipeline," *Washington Post*, June 11,
11   1998 at A-1.   89, 95, 124

12
     "100 Girls' Schools in Afghan Capital Are Ordered
13   Shut," *The New York Times*, June 17, 1998
14   (Associated Press).   86

15
     "Unocal Agrees to Massive Cleanup of Avila Beach;
16   Environment" *Los Angeles Times,* June 18, 1998 at A-1.   74

17
     Michael Hytha, "Final Unocal Payment for Pollution,"
18   *San Francisco Chronicle*, July 7, 1998 at A15.   74

19
     "Unocal OKs $43.8 Million Settlement," *San Francisco
20   Chronicle*, July 22, 1998 at A24.   73

21
     Nora Boustany, "Wretched Art They Amongst Women,"
22   *The Washington Post*, August 5, 1998.   87

23
     Mohammed Basheer, "Victorious Taliban Reopen
24   Bid for Recognition, Pipeline," *Agence France Presse*
25   August 11, 1998.   91

26

27

28

HEED 8/98

OTHER

AFL-CIO Executive Council, "Burma," February 19, 1997.   84

Shelley Alpern, "Another Burma? Unocal Joins Forces With Brutal Afghan Regime to Further Regional Oil Pipeline," *Franklin Research's Insight*, July 1998.   87, 88

Amnesty International, *Myanmar Portering & Forced Labour: Amnesty International's Concerns* (September 1996).   101, 111

Dennis Bernstein & Leslie Kean, "People of the Opiate: Burma's Dictatorship of Drugs," *The Nation* (N.Y.), December 16, 1996.   127, 128

Ed Bianchi, "The Lubicon Lake Cree," *Akwesasne Notes,* March 31, 1996.   118

"California, Connecticut and Vermont consider Burma Ban," available on the University of North Carolina Internet site ftp://sunsite.unc.edu/pub/academic/ political-science/freeburma/ba/. /Burma/ab2800.htm.   115

California Lawyer 1992-96.   52

California Public Interest Research Group (CALPIRG), *Crude Policy, Subsidies of the Oil Industry by California Taxpayers* 3 (December 1997).   70

Tony Clarke, *Dismantling Corporate Rule* 4 (Int'l Forum on Globalization, San Francisco 1996).   46

Conservation International, "Annual Report 1997" (1998). 78

"Corporate Brief, In-House Counsel," *The National Law Journal*, November 10, 1997 at 3.   132

Heida Diefenderfer, "Lubicon Cree Impoverished as

HEED 8/98

Multi-Nationals and Government Colonize Northern Alberta, *News From Indian Country,* August 15, 1997. 118

Joseph J. Drexler, OCAW Special Projects Director, "Remarks to the International Indigenous People's Tribunal in Conjunction with The Other Economic Summit (TOES)," Denver, June 19, 1997. 83

Earth Rights International (ERI) and Southeast Asia Information Network (SAIN), *Total Denial: A Report on the Yadana Pipeline Project in Burma* (1996). 79, 97, 106, 108, 109, 113, 114, 121, 122, 124

EDK Associates, *Corporate Irresponsibility: There Ought To Be Some Laws* (N.Y. 1996, available from the Preamble Center for Public Policy, Washington, D.C.). 36

The Feminist Majority Foundation, "Stop Gender Apartheid in Afghanistan!" available on Feminist Majority Internet web site at www.feminist.org. 85, 89

Richard L. Grossman & Frank T. Adams, *Taking Care of Business: Citizenship and the Charter of Incorporation* (1993). 40

Human Rights Watch/Asia, *Burma, Children's Rights and the Rule of Law,* (January 1997), available from Human Rights Watch's Internet site located at http://www.hrw.org.. 103, 104, 105

Human Rights Watch/Asia, *Human Rights Developments and the Need for Continued Pressure,* available from Human Rights Watch's Internet site www.hrw.org. 101, 102

Investor Responsibility Research Center, 1998 Company Report — E and E: 2, Unocal (May 11, 1998). 134

Joshua Karliner, *The Corporate Planet* ch. 6, (1998). 77

David C. Korten, *When Corporations Rule the World* (1995). 46

HEED 8/98

Representative George Miller, "Underpayment a Fueling at $2 Billion Taxpayers Scam," *Roll Call,* June 8, 1998.

Gregory Millman, "Troubling Projects, " *Infrastructure Finance*, February/March 1996.   106

Russell Mokhiber, "Soft on Crime," *Multinational Monitor* (1995) available on Internet site www.essential.org.   55

National Organization for Women, *The Day The Music Died: Women and Girls in Afghanistan*, Internet site at www.now.org/us-search/foundation.   128

"Oilwatch/NGO Declaration on Climate Change, Fossil Fuels and Public Funding," signed by nearly 200 environmental organizations on five continents (Kyoto, December 2, 1997).   76, 78

Physicians for Human Rights, *The Taliban's War on Women: A Health and Human Rights Crisis in Afghanistan* (Boston, Washington, D.C. 1998).   89, 95

Zohra Rasekh, MPH, et al., "Women's Health and Human Rights in Afghanistan," *Journal of the American Medical Association*, Abstracts, August 5, 1998.   87, 88

Lincoln Steffens, "New Jersey: A Traitor State," 24 *McClure's Magazine* 649, Part I April 1905, Part II May 1905.   43

Total, *The Yadana Gas Development Project* (1997).   78, 121

"Unocal Becomes A Company Without A Nation," 12 *Business Ethics* 6 (January/February 1998).   69, 80

Unocal Corp., *Annual Report 1997* (1998).   71

HEED 8/98

1
2   Unocal Corporation, Annual Report Securities Exchange
Commission Form 10-K (March 1998), available at
Internet site http://sec.yahoo.com/e/980331/ucl.html.   73, 75

3
4   Unocal www.unocal.com/. . ./96hesrpt/hestrust.htm.   74

5   Unocal Corporation, Annual Report 1997 (1998).   77, 80

6
7   Unocal Position Statement: "Proposed Central Asia
Pipeline Projects," (1998) available on Unocal Internet
8   site at www.unocal.com.   85, 90, 92

9
10   UNO/Unocal Afghan Training & Education Project
Cooperative Agreement, effective August 1, 1997,
11   Attachment C.   92

12
13   UNO/Unocal Afghan Training & Education Project
Cooperative Agreement, effective August 1, 1997.   92

14   Unocal, Constructive Engagement In Myanmar, Testimony
15   submitted to the U.S. Senate Banking Committee on S.
1511, May 22, 1996, by John Imle, President of Unocal
16   Corporation, available on the Unocal Internet site
17   (February 1998) www.unocal.com.   97, 126

18   Unocal, December 12, 1996, News Release, available
19   on Unocal Internet site www.unocal.com/uclnews/96htm/.   98

20   Unocal, "Unocal announces new Myanmar gas discovery,"
21   March 5, 1996, News Release, available on Unocal Internet
site www.unocal.com/uclnews/96htm/.   98
22

23   Unocal, Statement of Unocal Corporation for the Department
24   of Labor Report to Congress, February 1998, available
on Unocal web site www.unocal.com.   97, 105, 108, 115
25

26   Unocal, Commission for Justice and Peace, *Humanitarian
Report: Yadana Project* (1998), available on Unocal Internet
27   site at www.unocal.com/myanmar/timm.htm   108

28

HEED 8/98

1
2 Unocal, "Another side to economic development," Unocal Internet site at www.unocal.com/pep/pepintro.htm.   125

3 Unocal, "Developing Economies (Southeast and Central Asia)," Unocal Internet site at
4 www.unocal.com/pep/pepasia.htm.   125

5
6 Unocal, "Proxy Statement for the 1998 Annual Meeting of Stockholders," at 29 (April 20, 1998).   125

7
8 Unocal, www.unocal.com/myanmar/timm2.htm.   133

9 Unocal, www.unocal.com/myanmar/labor.htm.   133

10
   Unocal, www.unocal.com/myanmar/timm.htm.   133
11

12 Western Governors' Association, *Multilateral Agreement on Investment: Potential Effects on State & Local*
13 *Government* (April, 1997).   45

14
15 World Wildlife Fund, *Global 200 Ecoregions* (Draft, August 1997).   79

16
17 Jenna E. Ziman, "The Social and Environmental Costs of Oil Company Divestment from U.S. Refineries,"
18 *Multinational Monitor*, May 1997, available on Internet
19 site www.essential.org.   82

20
21
22
23
24
25
26
27
28

1

2

**Petition to the Attorney General of California
to Revoke the Corporate Charter of
The Union Oil Company of California (UNOCAL)**

3

4

5

6

**Submitted by the National Lawyers Guild
International Law Project for
Human, Economic & Environmental Defense (HEED)
on behalf of petitioners**

7

8

9

10

11

12

13

14

15

16

17

18

19

20

21

22

23

24

25

26

27

- Action Resource Center
- Alliance for Democracy of U.S.A.
- Alliance for Democracy of Austin, Texas
- Alliance for Democracy of San Fernando Valley, California
- Gloria Allred, individual
- Amazon Watch
- Asian/Pacific Gays and Friends
- Burma Forum Los Angeles
- Democracy Unlimited of
- Humboldt County, California
- Earth Island Institute
- Michael Feinstein, City Council Member, Santa Monica, California, individual
- Feminist Majority Foundation
- Free Burma Coalition
- Free Burma — No Petro-dollars for SLORC
- Global Exchange
- Randall Hayes, individual
- National Lawyers Guild of U.S.A.
- National Lawyers Guild of Los Angeles, San Diego, Santa Clara Valley and San Francisco
- National Organization for Women (NOW) National Organization for Women (NOW) of California
- Program on Corporations, Law and Democracy
- Project Maje
- Project Underground
- Rainforest Action Network
- Harvey Rosenfield, individual
- Surfers' Environmental Alliance
- Transnational Resource and Action Center

28

INTRODUCTION AND SUMMARY[1]

To the Attorney General of California:

Giant Corporations — by participating in and therefore warping elections, lawmaking, jurisprudence, and the education of a sovereign, self-governing people; by using wealth resulting from special privilege to influence political decisions in this and other countries; by coercing obedience via job blackmail; and by massive spending and propagandizing to mold public debate — are routinely engaged in the mechanics of the civil governing of this state.

Despite the fact that such corporate dominance is contrary to the most fundamental elements of this state's and this nation's plan of democratic government, and despite the fact that polling shows large majorities of Americans of all parties, ages, and races are extremely angry at corporate behavior and more than two-thirds favor government intervention against it,[2] many citizens today seem to fatalistically accept this state of affairs as inevitable even though, the truth is, it is of relatively recent invention. Moreover, the people of California and the United States still retain the legal authority to define what we want corporations to be and to require them to behave the way we want them to. The courts have consistently held that corporations are "mere creatures of the state," and as U.S. Supreme Court Justice White said in 1978 about corporations: "The state need not permit its own creation to consume it."

To redefine the corporation will be a daunting task, given the power of big business and given the last 100 years of special privileges granted to corporations by legislatures and courts. But the people of California, acting through you, our attorney general, do have one straightforward remedy already on the books that can accomplish much: The power to revoke a corporation's charter, that is, to dissolve the company and have its assets sold to others who will carry on a business more appropriately. We ask you to start with Unocal.

---

1 The text of the complaint, also referred to as the petition, contains the documented sources for the more general summary.

2 EDK Associates, Corporate Irresponsibility: There Ought To Be Some Laws (N.Y. 1996, available from the Preamble Center for Public Policy, Washington, D.C.).

HEED 8/98

Corporate repeat offenders.

Charter revocation is a particularly apt legal mechanism to deal with corporate repeat offenders. When large corporate violators, as contrasted with small businesses, pay fines, what they pay is often insignificant in relation to assets, and is flicked off the corporate suit merely as a cost of doing business rather than as a serious warning to change unlawful, anti-social corporate behavior. Unlike individuals who face tough "three-strikes-you're out" prosecutors, big corporations typically run decades-long rap sheets of criminal and civil violations. They are incorrigible recidivists. Yet they are rarely put out of business.

The evidence against Unocal.

This complaint, for example, alleges, on information and belief, that there is strong evidence for the attorney general to find that Unocal

- was principally responsible for the notorious 1969 oil blowout in the Santa Barbara Channel and after that went on year by year to grievously pollute air, land and water at multiple sites from San Francisco to Los Angeles — including the largest leak in California history, along the central coast;
- has been identified as a potentially responsible party at 82 "Superfund" or similar toxic sites;
- has committed hundreds of Occupational Safety and Health Act violations in the last twelve years;
- has treated U.S. workers unethically and unfairly;
- carries on ventures with foreign business partners in a fashion that makes the company complicit in and legally liable for their partners' unspeakable human rights violations against women, gays, laborers, villagers, ethnic minorities and indigenous peoples;
- has usurped political power and works to subvert U.S. foreign policy;
- and has engaged in a pattern of illegal deceptions of the courts, stockholders and the public.

At minimum, Unocal's record appears to involve hundreds of incidents and many thousands of victims — 18,000 alone in one incident in the San Francisco Bay Area — not to mention the vast numbers of women, villagers and ethnic minorities suffering severe human rights harms.

Corporations like Unocal claim legal rights as "persons" under the law, yet if they were real persons their many "strikes" would have put them "out" of social action permanently. It is hardly a radical or drastic notion that some corporations should be permanently prevented from doing harm. The state permanently revokes the privilege to do business of accountants, doctors, lawyers and others licensed by the state — hundreds of them every year. Why do corporations get special treatment?

The familiar, but ignored, tool of charter revocation.

The answer cannot be that charter revocation is an obscure or arcane legal mechanism, for it is a traditional and familiar one in all 50 states. Legal publishers routinely describe it in their manuals that keep lawyers up to date on the law. In California, the very same statutory words that authorize revocation of corporate charters also authorize revocation of governmental power unlawfully usurped, and those words have been used for the latter purpose scores of times over the years. We know that you, Mr. Attorney General, have an assistant specially assigned to handle all matters arising from this well-known statute.

Attorneys general and governors soft on corporate crime.

Why, then, are so few corporate charters revoked in California, and relatively few across the nation? The answer must be that the attorneys general are neglecting their duty to protect the public interest by ignoring the most effective corporate crime-fighting tool at their command. California has one of the strongest statutes on the books, mandating that "the attorney general *must* bring the action, whenever he has reason to believe" that a corporation has violated the law, "or when he is directed to do so by the governor." Yet our attorneys general and our governors have been soft on corporate crime, preferring to perpetuate the illusion that regulatory fines and occasional prosecutions are doing the job, while giving in to the corporate blackmail that "an unfriendly business climate" will drive companies out of the state — as if enforcing the law is unfriendly to business. The people of the state of California, and the legitimate businesses of the state, can no longer afford to pay this blackmail. The costs to our health, safety, jobs, unions, environment, human rights, economy, small businesses, quality of life and fair competition, are too great. Moreover, the statute does not give you discretion to ignore massive, well-referenced evidence presented to you by private parties such as that which we present to you here against Unocal. On this evidence, if necessary, a

1 court may compel you by a writ of mandamus to initiate revocation
   proceedings.

2   Furthermore, we point out that this is not a matter for political
3 partisanship or ideology.

4   The last significant corporate charter revocation action in California was filed in 1976 by conservative Republican Attorney General
5 Evelle Younger. When confronted with allegations that a private wa-
6 ter company in existence since 1909 was distributing possibly contaminated water to its customers — allegations much less serious than
7 many of those lodged against Unocal in this petition — he went to
8 court to revoke the company's charter despite the fact that the health
   authorities were also investigating the case. Because of the Attorney
9 General's suit and other legal actions, the company agreed to go out of
10 existence and have its assets purchased by a public water district that
   would upgrade its facilities.

11   Just months ago, the Republican attorney general of New York
12 went to court to revoke the charters of two non-profit corporations
   that allegedly had been producing false and deceptive information for
13 the tobacco industry about the links between smoking and health. That
14 case is pending.

15   In Alabama, a judge, elected to the bench as a Democrat but acting as a private citizen, has recently gone to court to revoke the corpo-
16 rate charters of all the major tobacco companies themselves doing
17 business in his state. Alabama law, unlike California law, does not
   require the approval of the attorney general.
18

19   **Relief requested.**
       We respectfully ask you, as an elected official sworn to be tough
20 on crime, to recognize your duty under the law, to rise to the standard
21 set by your predecessor Evelle Younger, by the attorney general of
   New York, and by the Alabama judge, and to initiate charter revoca-
22 tion proceedings against the Union Oil Company of California based
23 upon the evidence below. We further request that pending the outcome
24 of this proceeding you ask the court to appoint a receiver to take over
   and manage the business and affairs of the corporation. Finally, we
25 request that you ask the court to exercise its authority under the statute
26 to make such orders "as justice and equity require," specifically to
   guarantee full protection to jobs, workers, stockholders, unions, com-
27 munities, the environment, suppliers, customers, governmental enti-
28 ties, and the public interest. We are also providing a copy of this peti-

1 tion to the Governor of California and should it become necessary we
2 will call on him to direct you to initiate the proceedings we request.

3

4

5

6

7

8

9

10

11

12

13

14

15

16

17

18

19

20

21

22

23

24

25

26

27

28

I. Recalling that the People Are Sovereign Over Corporations

From the founding of the Massachusetts Bay Colony Company, to the forced break-up of Standard Oil in 1911, to the anti-trust prosecution of Microsoft Corporation today, the people's ability to create, dissolve and discipline the economic entities chartered within their borders has critically influenced life in America. The interaction between government and corporations has shaped the distribution of society's wealth, the quality of life, and the meaning of democracy itself.

The legal instrument which empowers companies to play a role in our democracy is the corporate charter. The charter, by which states incorporate economic enterprises and grant them special privileges, is one of the most powerful legal devices ever created. As the Temporary National Economic Committee of the Congress found in 1941, "[t]he principal instrument of the concentration of economic power and wealth has been the corporate charter with unlimited power."[3]

Carrying on common law principles which have existed "from the time whereof the memory of man runneth not to the contrary,"[4] state and federal courts have consistently recognized the authority of states, in the exercise of their sovereign police power, to revoke corporate charters. Yet few corporations today fear this sort of ultimate accountability for crimes and anti-social behavior, for now it is seldom even mentioned that corporate charters are legally revocable. Non-lawyers have had to remind the legal profession that this authority is still on the books.[5] This petition seeks to awaken the legal system from its historical amnesia by setting in motion the formal legal process to revoke a corporate charter and dissolve a corporation which is in many

---

3   77th Cong., 1st Sess., S.Doc. 35, TNEC, Final Report and Recommendations 28 (1941).

4   Wilmington City Ry. Co. v. People's Ry. Co., 47 A. 245 (1900).

5   Richard L. Grossman & Frank T. Adams, *Taking Care of Business: Citizenship and the Charter of Incorporation* (1993). The thesis of this pamphlet has been carried into action by the work of the Program on Corporations, Law and Democracy (POCLAD) which focuses on the fundamental relationship between the sovereign people and the subordinate corporate entities they create. Inspired by Grossman and Adams, law-

ways typical of the transnational behemoths of our time and which has a record of wrongdoing that cannot reasonably be ignored by the attorney general: the Union Oil Company of California which does business as "Unocal."[6]

II. THE HISTORY OF CONTROL OF CORPORATIONS

Originally, the states kept corporations subordinate through charters.

From the very beginning of our nation the power to grant existence to corporations has been vested in the individual states, each controlling activity within its own domain. Initially most corporations were chartered to build public works and conveniences. Some private corporations, however, were chartered for profit-making enterprises and were given special privileges in order to enhance their economic viability. At law, a corporation was classically defined as

> an artificial being, invisible, intangible, and existing only in contemplation of law. Being the mere creature of law, it possesses only those properties which the charter of its creation confers upon it, either expressly, or as incidental to its very existence. . . .[7]

Typically the companies were kept on a short leash, given life for

---

yers have now begun to refresh the springs of legal scholarship. The pioneering work is Thomas Linzey, "Awakening a Sleeping Giant: Creating a Quasi-Private Cause of Action for Revoking Corporate Charters in Response to Environmental Violations," 13 *Pace Environmental Law Review* 219, (1995); Thomas Linzey, "Killing Goliath: Defending Our Sovereignty and Environmental Sustainability Through Corporate Charter Revocation in Pennsylvania and Delaware," 6 *Dickinson Journal of Environmental Law & Policy* 31 (1997).

6   See Section V below for clarification of the relationship between the California entity "Union Oil Company of California" and the Delaware entity "Unocal Corporation."

7   *Trustees of Dartmouth College v. Woodward,* 17 U.S. (4 Wheat.) 518, 636-638 (1819).

a determined period of years and for narrow, public purposes.[8] Their charters were revocable, and were frequently revoked.

Corporations later won some important constitutional privileges.

In 1819 the Supreme Court ruled in *Trustees of Dartmouth College v. Woodward* [9] that the legislature of the state of New Hampshire could not reorganize Dartmouth College in violation of the original charter granted to the school's founder. *Dartmouth* held that a grant of incorporation is a "contract" and under the United States Constitution contracts cannot be impaired. In *Santa Clara County v. Southern Pacific Railroad*,[10] decided in 1886, the Fourteenth Amendment of the Constitution was held to protect the interests of corporations as "persons" benefiting from certain constitutional protections and rights enjoyed by natural persons under the Fourteenth Amendment while simultaneously possessing the privileges granted by incorporation. Without any discussion, debate or explanation, the Court applied to corporations the Fourteenth Amendment, which had been designed to protect blacks freed from slavery. The decision has long been subject to grave criticism for its lack of basis in law, history or logic.[11]

Then, in a "race to the bottom," states began competing with one another to loosen charter requirements, further eroding effective state control.

Pressured relentlessly by business to permit more charters, in the late Nineteenth Century legislatures began enacting "general incorporation laws" allowing any company to form for any lawful purpose

---

8   For a description and history of the restrictions see the scholarly opinion of Justice Brandeis in *Liggett Co. v. Lee*, 288 U.S. 517, 541 (1933) (Brandeis dissent).
9   *Dartmouth College*, *s*upra note 7.
10 118 U.S. 384 (1886).
11 See, *e.g.*, *Wheeling Steel Corp. v. Glander*, 337 U.S. 562, 576 (1949) (Douglas dissent) and *Connecticut General Co. v. Johnson*, 303 U.S. 77, 87 (1938) (Black dissent). In the latter, Justice Black wrote: "This Amendment sought to prevent discrimination by the states against classes or races. . . . Yet, of the cases in this Court in which the Fourteenth Amendment was applied during the first fifty years after its adoption, less than one-half of one percent invoked it in protection of the negro race, and more than fifty per cent asked that its benefits be extended to corporations." Id. at 89.

and to enjoy perpetual life. Soon, states were competing with one another to attract corporations and their tax revenues by removing all but the most elemental restrictions. Thus began the infamous "race to the bottom" that within a single generation ended the centuries long tradition of holding corporations to strict charters. The noted journalist Lincoln Steffens described in McClure's Magazine at the time how openly corrupt the process was, particularly in New Jersey. "She [New Jersey] not only licensed companies to do in other states what those states would not license; she licensed them to do in those other states what she would not let them do in Jersey. No our sister state was not prompted by any abstract consideration of right and wisdom. New Jersey sold us out for money."[12] Justice Brandeis described the phenomenon in his opinion in *Liggett v. Lee:*

> The removal by the leading industrial states of the limitations upon the size and powers of business corporations appears to have been due, not to their conviction that maintenance of the restrictions was undesirable in itself, but to the conviction that it was futile to insist upon them; because local restriction would be circumvented by foreign [out of state] incorporation. Indeed, local restriction seemed worse than futile. Lesser states, eager for the revenue derived from the traffic in charters, had removed safeguards from their own incorporation laws. Companies were early formed to provide charters for corporations in states where the cost was lowest and the laws least restrictive. The states joined in advertising their wares. The race was one not of diligence but of laxity. [13]

Some conservative economists today dispute that this was a "race to the bottom," arguing that corporate profits increased as controls loosened. But the profit data do not show a causal link between the removal of controls and higher profits. More importantly, the data ignore the increase in usurpation of ungranted powers, corporate lawlessness, anti-social and undemocratic behavior as states let go of the reins.

---

12 Lincoln Steffens, "New Jersey: A Traitor State," 24 *McClure's Magazine* 649, Part I April 1905, Part II May 1905.

13 *Liggett,* supra note 8 at 557.

HEED 8/98

Government resorted to the "regulatory state" as an alternative way to control corporate behavior, but business largely escaped that through sophisticated political and legal counterattack.

As the states eased restraints on charters, they and the federal government did, however, attempt to guide corporate behavior through direct legislation and numerous new administrative agencies. Reflecting the Populist movement in the late Nineteenth Century, the Progressive era early in the Twentieth, and the New Deal of the 1930s, extensive laws were adopted at all levels putatively to prevent monopolies, promote economic competition, safeguard health, empower workers, protect consumers, cleanse politics, and more. Actually, however, the Populists' tough program to subordinate corporate power to the will of the people was eroded by Progressive and New Deal regulatory "protections" that really protected large corporations while they pursued maximization of production and reduced the people's expectations for basic change. Despite periodic political cycles of "deregulation," this regulatory state continues in the last half of the Twentieth Century as part of the fabric of American life. Important new regulations have been promulgated in recent decades on matters sometimes crucial to the quality of life and social justice but many are destined to fail to get at the root of the problem: corporate power over sovereign, democratic people.

Business did not take the rise of the regulatory state lightly. It counterattacked with both political and legal weapons. Politically, business worked and still works assiduously to rid itself of the regulatory watchdogs, or at least to remove their teeth, and then to use them for protection. By financing two-party-only elections, and by direct lobbying, the business community has for years generally dominated legislators and captured administrative agencies. Corporations essentially have followed the advice of Richard Olney, President Grover Cleveland's Attorney General. Olney told railroad executives not to resist the creation of a regulatory commission because it could "be of great use" to them, "satisfy[ing] the popular clamor for government supervision of railroads, at the same time that the supervision is almost entirely nominal."[14] (Olney is also remembered for representing a private railroad client at the same time that he served as Attorney General and ordered federal troops to attack railway workers in the bloody Pullman Strike of 1884.)

---

14   Quoted in Kenneth Culp Davis, *Administrative Law Text* 6 (3d ed. 1972).

HEED 8/98

Legally, the corporate counterattack first blunted the regulatory state by claiming violations of "substantive due process" rights under the Fourteenth and Fifth Amendments. The doctrine was ushered in by *Lochner v. New York* [15] when the Supreme Court read into the due process clause of the Constitution an implicit laissez-faire economic policy. Under the doctrine the Supreme Court struck down more than 200 economic regulations.[16] A Fortune Magazine article declared approvingly in 1936 that the doctrine had worked "to insure to individual businessmen complete freedom from state regulation other than that which the Supreme Court held to be a proper exercise of governmental power." [17] The next year, however, in *West Coast Hotel Co. v. Parrish*, [18] under the economic and political pressure of the New Deal, the Court abandoned the substantive due process doctrine.

After *West Coast Hotel*, many government regulations were upheld that would have been invalidated earlier. But big business did not give up. It energetically and successfully stepped up claims to other constitutional rights originally intended for individuals, particularly First Amendment rights to free commercial and political speech, Fourth Amendment rights against searches, and certain Fifth Amendment rights protecting criminal defendants, property, and liberty interests like reputation. "Taken together, these Bill of Rights assertions represent a bold new challenge to government regulation. . . . [they] now form a substantive due process shield for corporations, reminiscent of the Fourteenth amendment shield extant in the Lochner era. The current judicial era is one of corporate substantive due process."[19]

Corporations today operate out of control as private governments, more powerful than nation-states.

Today, transnational corporations, operating alone as well as through supranational trade organizations and agreements, have a

---

15   198 U.S. 45 (1905).
16   Carl J. Mayer, "Personalizing the Impersonal: Corporations and the Bill of Rights," 41 *Hastings L.J.* 577, 589 (1990).
17   Quoted in Mayer, supra note 16 at 590.
18   300 U.S. 379 (1937).
19   Mayer, supra note 16 at 620, 662.

greater ability to circumvent state power than ever before.[20] Indeed, 50 of the 100 largest economies in the world are not nations but transnational corporations, and merely 500 corporations control 70 percent of global trade.[21] They have the power to run or ruin foreign economies, topple foreign governments, uproot cultural traditions overnight, threaten whole races of indigenous peoples, and destroy the global biosphere upon which the survival of future generations depends.[22]

The de facto reality, as Professor Arthur Miller concluded in 1968, is that modern day corporations have become entities unto themselves; a privately owned company "can be validly termed a 'private' government' whose power is not responsible or accountable to anyone."[23] The ability of private, for-profit corporations to control the international economy, influence domestic political and economic decisions and violate their charters without fear of significant punishment creates an urgent legal need for the resuscitation of meaningful state control of corporate activities.

Charter revocation, though ignored, remains intact as a legal remedy against corporate power.

Despite the *Dartmouth* and *Santa Clara* decisions, despite the legislative "race to the bottom" resulting in a new era of lax charters, despite "substantive due process" and First, Fourth and Fifth Amendment legal shields for corporations, the legal door never closed on charter revocation. After *Dartmouth* the Supreme Court distinguished the states' obligation not to interfere with corporate contracts from their affirmative right to govern corporate charters. In *Bank of Augusta v. Earle* the Court explained that the contract-making power of a

---

20 State and national sovereignty both are being yielded to international organizations created at the behest of, and dominated by, transnational corporations interested single-mindedly in promoting global trade. See Western Governors' Association, *Multilateral Agreement on Investment: Potential Effects on State & Local Government* (April, 1997); Robert Stumberg, *The New Supremacy of Trade: NAFTA Rewrites the Status of States* (Center for Policy Alternatives, Washington, D.C., September, 1993); and, e.g., Nancy Dunne, "Anger Over WTO Turtle Ruling," *Financial Times* (London, March 14, 1998) at 3.

21 Tony Clarke, *Dismantling Corporate Rule* 4 (Int'l Forum on Globalization, San Francisco 1996).

22 See generally, David C. Korten, *When Corporations Rule the World* (1995).

23 Arthur Miller, *The Supreme Court and American Capitalism* 15 (1968).

corporation is circumscribed by the limitations contained in its charter:

> [I]t may be safely assumed that a corporation can make no contracts, and do no acts either within or without the state which creates it, except such as are authorized by its charter; and those acts must also be done, by such officers or agents, and in such manner as the charter authorizes. [24]

The corporation's obligation to its charter is also an obligation to the state of incorporation. No matter a corporation's size or the scope of its activities, the special privileges it enjoys are granted by the sovereign authority of the state that incorporated it:

> [F]ranchises are special privileges conferred by government upon individuals, and which do not belong to the citizens of the country, generally, or by common right. It is essential to the character of a franchise that it should be a grant from the sovereign authority, and in this country no franchise can be held which is not derived from the law of the state. [25]

By the time of *Standard Oil of New Jersey v. United States,* [26] a 1911 decision in which the Supreme Court upheld the revocation of a petroleum trust's charter, corporations chartered for business in the United States had already accumulated more capital than existed in any other nation. In the opinion the danger posed by unchecked corporate activity was juxtaposed to slavery as one of the defining issues in our nation's development, aspirations and prosperity:

> All who recall the condition of the country in 1890 will remember that there was everywhere, among the people generally, a deep feeling of unrest. The nation had been rid of human slavery—fortunately, as all now feel—but the conviction was universal that the country was in real danger from another kind of slavery sought to be fastened on the American people: namely, the slavery that would result from aggregations of capital in the hands of a few individuals and corporations controlling, for their own profit and advantage exclusively, the entire business of the country,

---

24 38 U.S. (13 Pet.) 519-520, (1839).
25 Id. at 595.
26 221 U.S. 1 (1911).

HEED 8/98

including the production and sale of the necessities of life.[27]

The Supreme Court reasoned that the individual freedoms which our government is designed to preserve depend for their existence upon a democracy free of political and economic domination by an uncontrolled elite. State and federal high court decisions have consistently related charter revocation to the most fundamental precepts of our national identity because unchecked corporate power has been deemed to be inherently undemocratic.

In 1933, Justice Louis Brandeis, who was of the view that "the citizens of each state are still masters of their destiny"[28] when it came to setting the terms on which corporations would be allowed to do business wholly within the state, told of the evils that justified the citizens' assertion of sovereignty over business:

> The prevalence of the corporation in America has led men of this generation to act, at times, as if the privilege of doing business in corporate form were inherent in the citizen; and has led them to accept the evils attendant upon the free and unrestricted use of the corporate mechanism as if these evils were the inescapable price of civilized life and, hence, to be borne with resignation. Throughout the greater part of our history a different view prevailed. Although the value of this instrumentality in commerce and industry was fully recognized, incorporation for business was commonly denied long after it had been freely granted for religious, educational and charitable purposes. It was denied because of fear. Fear of encroachment upon the liberties and opportunities of the individual. Fear of the subjection of labor to capital. Fear of monopoly. Fear that the absorption of capital by corporations, and their perpetual life, might bring evils. . . .There was a sense of some insidious menace inherent in large aggregations of capital, particularly when held by corporations.[29]

And Justice Brandeis warned ominously of the threat to democracy that justifies sovereign control of corporations:

---

27 Id. at 83.
28 *Liggett Co. v. Lee*, 288 U.S. 517, 580 (1933) (Brandeis dissent).
29 Id. at 548-549 (1933) (footnotes omitted).

HEED 8/98

Able and discerning scholars have pictured for us the economic and social results of thus removing all limitations upon the size and activities of business corporations and of vesting in their managers vast powers once exercised by stockholders—results not designed by the states and long unsuspected. . . . Through size, corporations, once merely an efficient tool employed by individuals in the conduct of private business, have become an institution—an institution which has brought such concentration of economic power that so-called private corporations are sometimes able to dominate the state. The typical business corporation of the last century, owned by a small group of individuals, managed by their owners, and limited in size by their personal wealth, is being supplanted by huge concerns in which the lives of tens or hundreds of thousands of employees and the property of tens or hundreds of thousands of investors are subjected, through the corporate mechanism, to the control of a few men. Ownership has been separated from control; and this separation has removed many of the checks which formerly operated to curb the misuse of wealth and power. And as ownership of the shares is becoming continually more dispersed, the power which formerly accompanied ownership is becoming increasingly concentrated in the hands of a few. The changes thereby wrought in the lives of the workers, of the owners and of the general public, are so fundamental and far-reaching as to lead these scholars to compare the evolving "corporate system" with the feudal system; and to lead other men of insight and experience to assert that this "master institution of civilized life" is committing it to the rule of a plutocracy.[30]

Although this opinion was written in dissent in 1933, subsequent Supreme Court decisions have never disputed Brandeis's premise that states need not tolerate corporate behavior that threatens democracy. This is true even at the hard center of the new constitutional shield of corporate rights represented by *First National Bank of Boston v. Belotti.*[31] In a 5 to 4 decision, the Court in *Belotti* forbade states from prohibiting corporate speech about ballot propositions submitted to the voters. It rejected as "extreme" the argument "that corporations, as

---

30 Id. at 564-565 (1933) (footnotes omitted).
31 435 U.S. 765 (1978).

creatures of the State, have only those rights granted them by the State," finding that the corporations have other rights under the constitution as well, such as the First Amendment rights in question. Yet the Court never questioned that corporations are "creatures of the state" and could be controlled by them. It declared only that the particular state regulation went too far. Had the state shown enough evidence of a corporate threat to "the confidence of the people in the democratic process and the integrity of government," it appears that the regulation would have been upheld:

> According to appellee, corporations are wealthy and powerful and their views may drown out other points of view. If appellee's arguments were supported by record or legislative findings that corporate advocacy threatened imminently to undermine democratic processes, thereby denigrating rather than serving First Amendment interests, these arguments would merit our consideration.[32]

The dissents in *Belotti* by Justices White and Rehnquist opined that enough evidence of the threat had already been demonstrated, or need not be demonstrated, to uphold the state's regulation. Justice White commented:

> Corporations are artificial entities created by law for the purpose of furthering certain economic goals. In order to facilitate the achievement of such ends, special rules relating to such matters as limited liability, perpetual life, and the accumulation, distribution, and taxation of assets are normally applied to them. States have provided corporations with such attributes in order to increase their economic viability and thus strengthen the economy generally. It has long been recognized, however, that the special status of corporations has placed them in a position to control vast amounts of economic power which may, if not regulated, dominate not only the economy but also the very heart of our democracy, the electoral process. . . . The State need not permit its own creation to consume it. [33]

For his part, Chief Justice Rehnquist threw doubt on *Santa Clara County's* 1886 grant of personhood to corporations under the Four-

---

32 Id. at 789.
33 Id. at 809 (White dissent).

teenth Amendment, then quoted *Dartmouth College's* definition of a corporation as a "mere creature of law" possessing only those powers conferred by charter or necessarily incidental to its existence, and stated:

> I can see no basis for concluding that the liberty of a corporation to engage in political activity with regard to matters having no material effect on its business is necessarily incidental to the purposes for which the Commonwealth permitted these corporations to be organized or admitted within its boundaries.[34]

In sum, the legal situation at the end of the Twentieth Century is the same as it was at the beginning of the Nineteenth: Corporations are "mere creatures of law." Within the bounds of the constitution, the state gives them life, can regulate it, and can take it away.

The political branches have a duty to exercise the authority recognized by the courts. Woodrow Wilson, in his inaugural address as Governor of New Jersey, aptly summed up the power and responsibility of the states:

> A corporation exists, not of natural right, but only by license of law, and the law, if we look at the matter in good conscience, is responsible for what it creates .... If law is at liberty to adjust the general conditions of society itself, it is at liberty to control these great instrumentalities which nowadays, in so large part, determine the character of society.[35]

---

34 Id. at 828 (Rehnquist dissent).
35 Quoted in *Liggett Co. v. Lee*, 288 U.S. 517, 560, n. 37 (1933) (Brandeis dissent).

HEED 8/98

III. THE REMEDY IGNORED: QUO WARRANTO

Statutes to revoke corporate charters are on the books in every state.

The notion that the state may terminate a business that is harming the public is hardly a radical one. Doctors, lawyers, dry cleaners, accountants, beauticians, and others in the learned and practical professions can be permanently put out of business for their misbehavior.[36] Banks can be seized by the state and liquidated.[37] Insurance companies may have their certificates of authority revoked.[38] All fifty states and the District of Columbia have statutes providing for revocation of corporate charters.[39] The statutes codify the English common law writ of *quo warranto*, a Twelfth century English term of Latin and Frankish origin, meaning *by what authority*. The writ allows the attorney general to demand that the corporation show in a judicial proceeding by what authority it continues to exist. Courts have consistently held

---

36 See, e.g., California Business & Professions Code § 2227 (revocation of physicians' licenses), § 6078 (attorneys), § 9594 (dry cleaners), § 5100 (accountants), § 7403 (barbers and cosmetologists). In recent years, an average of 92 doctors, 102 lawyers, and 16 accountants per year have had their licenses revoked or surrendered them under threat of revocation. Figures compiled from letters from Medical Board of California and California Board of Accounting on file with petitioners' counsel, and from *California Lawyer* 1992-96.

37 See, e.g., California Financial Code § 3100 allowing the Commissioner of Banks to seize and liquidate any bank that has violated "its articles or any law of this state" or any bank that is "conducting its business in an unsafe or unauthorized manner."

38 See, e.g., California Insurance Code § 704.5 authorizing the Insurance Commissioner to revoke operating authority for insurance companies if any person with 10% or more of the stock has been convicted or theft, larceny, mail fraud, or violation of any securities or insurance statute.

39 The statutes are collected in Thomas Linzey, "Awakening a Sleeping Giant: Creating a Quasi-Private Cause of Action for Revoking Corporate Charters in Response to Environmental Violations," 13 *Pace Environmental Law Review* 219, 223, n. 15 (1995). Linzey subsequently added to his 49 state collection Alaska Corporations and Associations Code § 10.06.635.

that certain acts of wrongdoing clearly warrant charter revocation. Judges have upheld revocation as a remedy for "misuse" or "nonuse" of the corporate charter, "unlawful acts," "fraud," "willful abuse of chartered privileges," "usurpation of powers," "improper neglect of responsibility," "excess of power," "mistake in the exercise of an acknowledged power" and "failure to fulfill design and purpose."

A single act of unlawfulness is enough to trigger charter revocation.

A single act of wrongdoing is enough. For example, corporations have been held dissolvable for failing to lay railroad tracks by a date promised,[40] joining other companies to monopolize sugar[41] conducting fraudulent real estate practices,[42] putting out false advertising,[43] serving polluted water to customers,[44] running baseball games on Sundays,[45] paying members of the president's family excessive salaries,[46] self-dealing,[47] and for the corporate president being convicted four times in a year of illegally selling alcohol.[48]

Attorneys General can be compelled to act to revoke corporate charters.

Significantly, most state courts agree that an attorney general may be compelled by a writ of mandamus to file a quo warranto action where a private grievance or public harm has been shown. While the discretion of prosecutors whether or not to bring actions is normally given wide berth, both the ancient common law and some state statutes impose a mandatory duty upon the attorney general to bring a quo

---

40 *People v. Broadway Railroad* 26 N.E. 961 (N.Y. 1891).
41 *People v. North River Sugar Refining Co.,* 24 N.E. 834 (N.Y. 1890).
42 *State v Cartelle Corp.* 341 N.E. 2d 223 (N.Y. 1975).
43 *People v. Abbott Maintenance Corp., 201 N.Y.S.2d 895 (1960).*
44 *Commonwealth ex. rel. Elkin v. Potter County Water Co.,* 61 A. 1099 (Pa 1905).
45 *Commonwealth ex. rel. Woodruff v. American Baseball Club of Philadelphia ,* 138 A. 497 (Pa. 1927).
46 *Commonwealth ex. rel. Woods v. United States Annuity Society,* 154 A. 24 (Pa . 1931).
47 *Southerland ex. rel. Snider v. Decimo Club, Inc.,* 142 A. 786 (Del. Ch. 1928).
48 *Craven v. Fifth Ward Republican Club, Inc.,* 146 A.2d 400 (Del. Ch. 1958).

warranto action when proper evidence is presented that a corporation is violating the law.[49] According to a leading, current treatise, "it is generally accepted that the discretion of an attorney general in refusing to bring quo warranto is not an arbitrary discretion but subject to mandamus if refused." [50] This is also the law in California, as discussed later in this petition.

The regulatory state has obscured the quo warranto remedy, but a revival is at hand.

The rise of the regulatory state in the Twentieth Century, with its extensive legislation and administrative regulations, has obscured the remedy of quo warranto. The existence of criminal or civil penalties for particular offenses does not abridge the state's authority to revoke charters.[51] A state's attorney general may file an action in quo warranto without exhausting other legal remedies. But the public generally is not aware of this, and corporate lawyers and attorneys general do not want to remind them. Most of us proceed as if the state is limited to fighting corporate abuses one pollutant at a time, one layoff at a time, one human rights violation at a time. This has systematically tilted the playing field in favor of giant corporations. Unethical companies string out long patterns of abuse over many years, fighting government enforcement actions one at a time, "capturing" the agencies that regulate them, and paying usually small fines as part of the cost of doing business. Attorneys general and other prosecutors tout each iso-

---

49 See, e.g., *People ex rel. Raster v. Healy,* 82 N.E. 599 (Ill. 1907), *State ex rel. Evans v. Brotherhood of Friends,* 247 P.2d 787 (Wa. 1952), *State v. Village of Kent,* 104 N.W. 948 (Minn. 1905), *Bouch v. Alger Circuit Judge,* 124 N.W. 532 (Mich. 1910).

50 Chester J. Antieau, *The Practice of Extraordinary Remedies* § 4.15 (1987).

51 "There can be no doubt that a corporation may be proceeded against by quo warranto for a misuse or perversion of the franchise conferred upon it by the State, notwithstanding [that] its officers and agents may at the same time be amenable to the criminal law for offense committed by them in the perversion of such franchise [citation omitted]. Speaking through Mr. Justice Simpson we made it clear that a penalty provided in a penal statute for those who refuse to enforce it [does] not mean that that is the exclusive "remedy" , [and it should not] preclude the attorney general from proceeding against a corporation . . . with a view to prohibit the misuse of a franchise granted by the State." *Woodruff,* supra note 45, 500-501.

lated victory. The public is shammed into believing that government is trying to govern corporations when in fact the giant recidivist corporations have figured out how to make their anti-social acts tolerated by society. Quo warranto is the one remedy that can cut through the very root of this corporate wrongdoing rather than merely trim its branches. An attorney general who is committed to state sovereignty and intent on combating the most serious, costly crime, which is corporate crime,[52] should understand that *quo warranto* is the most effective tool available.

Attorneys general once knew this well. They did not hesitate to use the charter revocation tool against huge corporate interests such as the sugar trusts[53] and oil companies.[54] Indeed, as in the 1911 *Standard Oil* case[55] where a U.S. Attorney General dissolved a giant company, the federal anti-trust laws have continued all through this century as a familiar instance of the legal power to revoke corporate charters. Vigorous anti-trust enforcement is now in decline, but the decline of charter revocations at the state level came first as the regulatory state grew. Attorneys general put away the effective tool of *quo warranto* for big business; they became soft on big business. However, they did not, and do not today, hesitate to draw this particular arrow from their quivers, string it, and send it home when the target is some small, unpopular, or socially marginal enterprise, such as a segregationist group,[56] a political club illegally selling alcoholic beverages,[57] a trade school cheating on student loan funds,[58] a company selling floor waxing machines via sharp practices,[59] or a company promoting lewd magazines and "man/boy love."[60]

---

52 Russell Mokhiber, "Soft on Crime," *Multinational Monitor* (1995) available on Internet site www.essential.org.

53 See, *e.g.*, *People v. North River Sugar Ref. Co.*, 24 N.E. 834 (1890); *Havemeyer v. Superior Court of the City and County of San Francisco*, 84 Cal. 327 (1890).

54 See, *e.g.*, *Standard Oil of New Jersey v. United States*, 221 U.S. 1 (1911).

55 Id.

56 *Young v. Nat'l Association for Advancement of White People, Inc.*, 109 A.2d 29 (Del. 1954).

57 *Craven v. Fifth Ward Republican Club, Inc.*, 146 A.2d 400 (Del. 1958).

58 *People v. Oliver Schools*, 619 N.Y.S. 911 (1994).

59 *People v. Abbott Maintenance Corp.*, 201 N.Y.S. 895 (1960), aff'd 9 N.Y.S. 2d 761 (1961).

60 *People v. Zymurgy*, 649 N.Y.S. 2d 662 (1996).

In addition, attorneys general very frequently employ their *quo warranto* statutes to challenge the right of public officials to hold office or municipal governments' right to annex land, for the very same statutory words that authorize challenge to corporations to show "by what authority" they continue in existence also authorize the challenge to public officers to show "by what authority" they hold office or land. In California, the *quo warranto* statute, *Code of Civil Procedure* § 803, has been litigated dozens of times, and the Attorney General's office has written scores of official legal opinions on it, the majority in cases not involving corporations.[61] The California attorney general has a deputy attorney assigned to specialize in all cases under this statute, as well as several pages on the official web site devoted solely to quo warranto.[62] So the attorney general knows the statute well, and uses it, but inexplicably fails to use it against corporate violators.

One California attorney general in recent decades did use the statute in a significant case against serious corporate harm. Conservative Republican Attorney General Evelle Younger went to court in 1976 to force forfeiture of the franchise of a company supplying allegedly impure water to customers in Alameda County,[63] a case involving much less extensive harm than that alleged against Unocal in this petition.

There is encouraging news that a revival of *quo warranto* for serious corporate harm is at hand. The New York State attorney general has taken action to dissolve two non-profit corporations that he alleges illegally serve the cause of tobacco industry while posing as scientific research organizations.[64] The fact that his targets are non-profit corporations is immaterial, as the non-profit revocation statute is identical in pertinent respects to the for-profit corporations revocation statute. His petition to the court asserts that the corporations must

---

61 See annotations to § 803 in Deerings California Codes.

62 Internet http://caag.state.ca.us./.See Opinion Unit, Quo Warranto, Nature of the Remedy. The pages emphasize the use of quo warranto against public officeholders, with barely a mention of its history or use against corporations.

63 *Citizens Utilities Co. of California v. Superior Court of Alameda County*, 56 Cal. App. 3d 399 (1976), discussed below.

64 *People v. Council for Tobacco Research, U.S.A., Inc. and The Tobacco Institute, Inc.*, (filed April 30, 1998, Supreme Court of New York, N.Y. Courts, Index No. 107479/98).

be dissolved because they obtained their charters by fraudulently representing their purposes to be scientific and objective, they persisted in this deception of the public over the years, and this activity exceeded the authority conferred upon them by law.

Then, in June of 1998, an Alabama judge, acting as a private citizen under an Alabama statute that allows any individual without the permission of the attorney general to initiate *quo warranto* proceedings, sued six major tobacco companies themselves, asking state courts to revoke their charters to do business in Alabama on the ground that they are causing minors to consume and become addicted to "lethal tobacco products."[65]

This present petition on Unocal offers the attorney general of California the opportunity to take the next step in this revival of effective law enforcement.

---

65 *William J. Wynn ex rel. State of Alabama v. Phillip Morris et. al.* (Circuit Court, Jefferson County, Case No. CY 98-3295, June 6, 1998.)

HEED 8/98

IV. CHARTER REVOCATION IN CALIFORNIA

The statutes authorize revocation of corporate charters.

Corporate charters have been revocable through quo warranto in California ever since California became a state. The procedure is codified today in two separate statutes,[66] each providing independent and concurrent authority for the attorney general to act:

Code of Civil Procedure §803 provides in pertinent part:

> An action may be brought by the attorney-general, in the name of the people of this state, upon his own information, or upon a complaint of a private party... against any corporation ... which usurps, intrudes into, or unlawfully holds or exercises any franchise, within this state. And the attorney-general must bring the action, whenever he has reason to believe that any such office or franchise has been usurped, intruded into, or unlawfully held or exercised by any person, or when he is directed to do so by the governor.

In addition, *California Corporations Code* §1801 (formerly §4690) authorizes similar action. It provides, in pertinent part:

> (a) The Attorney General may bring an action against any domestic corporation or purported domestic corporation in the name of the people of this state, upon the Attorney General's own information or upon complaint of a private party, to procure a judgment dissolving the corporation and annulling, vacating or forfeiting its corporate existence upon any of the following grounds:
>
> (1) The corporation has seriously offended against any provision of the statutes regulating corporations.
>
> (2) The corporation has fraudulently abused or usurped corporate privileges or powers. ....

---

66 In addition, charters may be revoked specifically for violation of the state anti-trust laws and for violation of the Automobile Dealers Anti-coercion Act. Business & Professions Code §§ 16752, 18410.

The constitutionality of the statutes is unquestioned.[67] They operate concurrently[68] and, under the standard canon of construction relating to statutes *in pari materia* (on the same subject), they are to be interpreted together as a harmonious scheme.

The state supreme court is adamant that corporations are but creatures of the state.

The California Supreme Court has been as adamant as the U.S. Supreme Court and the high courts of other states in upholding the statutory remedy of quo warranto against errant corporations. In *The People ex rel. Attorney-General v. The Dashaway Association,*[69] the California court declared:

> Corporations are creatures of the law, and when they fail to perform duties which they were incorporated to perform, and in which the public have an interest, or do acts which are not authorized or are forbidden them to do, the state may forfeit their franchises and dissolve them by an information in the nature of quo warranto. The principle of a forfeiture is that the franchise is a trust; and the terms of the charter are conditions of the trust, and if any one of the conditions of the trust be violated, it will work a forfeiture of the charter. . . . The grant of corporate franchises is always subject to the implied condition that they will not be abused.

The court went on to enunciate two "great classes" of forfeiture:

> 1. Cases of perversion; as where a corporation does an act inconsistent with the nature and destructive of the ends and purposes of the grant. In such cases, unless the perversion is such as to amount to an injury to the public, who are interested in the franchise, it will not work a forfeiture. 2. Cases of usurpation; as where a corporation exercises a power which it has no right to exercise. In this last case the question of forfeiture is not dependent, as in the former, upon any interest or injury to the public.[70]

67 *Citizens Utilities Company of California v. The Superior Court of Alameda County*, 56 Cal. App. 3d, 399, 405 (1976).
68 Id.
69 84 Cal. 114, 117 (1890).
70 Id. at 119-220.

Many multinational corporations today belong to both of these "classes." Since the time of the *Dashaway* decision corporate power has grown exponentially to the point where corporate entities exercise power across borders, in ways which supersede state control. Not only are multiple acts of public "perversion" being routinely committed, these companies, which begin as domestic corporations, are "cases of usurpation," exercising powers which have not been given to them through a democratic process but which have been grasped through economic dominance.

A single unlawful act is enough to trigger revocation proceedings.

As in other states, California courts have held that charters are revocable even for a single act of abuse. Monopolizing the sugar market, supplying impure water to customers, or delaying a street car track for six years, for example, have each triggered legal action to forfeit charters.

Thus, in *Havemeyer v. Superior Court of the City and County of San Francisco,*[71] a corporation was found to have "grossly abused" its corporate franchise by maintaining a monopoly of refined sugar. Judgment of forfeiture of its charter and the imposition of a fine followed. The Supreme Court remarked:

> To guard the public interest and vindicate justice is the distinctive purpose of this proceeding by the attorney general; to maintain that a corporation, as being but a creature of the law, must obey the law—cannot be permitted to violate it with impunity; that its stockholders must respect the obligation they assume to the public when they sought and accepted their franchise at the hands of the public; that they must observe the policy upon which the commercial police power of the state proceeds—the policy which, notoriously disfavoring restraint of trade, absolutely forbids corporations to embark in monopoly in an article classed among the necessaries of human life—these features characterize this as a case of grave public interest, and one in the vindication of which the court is bound to employ all the powers

---

71   84 Cal. 327 (1890).
72   Id. at 356.

HEED 8/98

provided by the law, one of which is the power to appoint a receiver of the estate and effects of the delinquent corporation.[72]

In *Citizens Utilities Co. of California v. Superior Court of Alameda County,*[73] where a private water company in existence since 1909 was alleged to be supplying polluted water to its customers, the Court of Appeal noted that the Corporations Code authorizes the attorney general

to bring an action to dissolve and forfeit the existence of a corporation that has seriously offended against a provision of the statutes regulating corporations, has fraudulently abused or usurped corporate privileges or powers, or has violated any provision of law by any act or default that is a ground of forfeiture of corporate existence. . . . We conclude, therefore, that quo warranto may properly be invoked to oust petitioner of its franchise upon a cause of action alleging that it is furnishing to consumers water that has become impure, unwholesome and unpotable.[74]

And in *The People ex rel. Warfield v. Sutter Street Railway Co,*[75] the Supreme Court upheld the forfeiture of a corporate franchise to run a streetcar on Bush Street in San Francisco, on the ground that the corporation was testing track in Bush Street for six years in a sham operation to force the public onto its Sutter Street line.

Existence of other remedies irrelevant to a revocation action.
The revocation authority of *Code of Civil Procedure* §803 and *Corporations Code* §1801 stand independently of other remedies against law-breaking corporations.

[T]he availability of other remedies does not preclude the

---

73 56 Cal. App. 3d 399 (1976). The court stayed the attorney general's action until the investigation by the Public Utilities Commission could be finished. The litigation and related lawsuits were dropped shortly after the court's decision when Citizens Utilities Company agreed to be taken over by the public Alameda County Water District which purchased its assets and laid plans to upgrade the facilities. Greg Hartman, "ACWD Reaches Settlement in Water Fight with Citizens," *The Argus* (Fremont, California), March 26, 1976 at 1.
74 Id. at 405, 407.
75 117 Cal. 604 (1897).

statutory proceeding in the nature of quo warranto. . . . Code of Civil Procedure 803 enjoins on the Attorney General the duty of bringing actions for the forfeiture of corporate franchises whenever he has reason to believe they are unlawfully held or exercised. It is a preventative remedy addressed to preventing a continuing exercise of an authority unlawfully asserted rather than to correcting what has already been done under that authority. . . . Accordingly, quo warranto has been held to be the proper remedy by which a state may proceed to oust a corporation of its franchise rights, notwithstanding the fact that the corporation might be punished by an assessment of the penalty provided by law in a criminal prosecution.[76]

The Attorney General can be compelled to bring an action.

In California, as in most other jurisdictions, the attorney general has a mandatory duty to bring a quo warranto action in a proper case. *Code of Civil Procedure* §803 provides:

And the attorney-general *must* bring the action, whenever he has reason to believe that any such office or franchise has been usurped, intruded into, or unlawfully held or exercised by any person, or when he is directed to do so by the governor. [Emphasis added.]

The words "must bring the action" are plain on their face and require no interpretation. They are mandatory in the law. They apply in the two instances of first, "whenever he has reason to believe [that a violation has occurred]," and second, "when he is directed to do so by the governor." He has no more discretion to ignore evidence of a violation than he has to ignore a directive by the governor.

Naturally, the attorney general retains the discretion to judge when he "has reason to believe," and the courts will give that discretion considerable deference. In *City of Campbell v. Stanley Mosk*,[77] the Court of Appeal held that: "to justify court intervention, the abuse of discretion by the Attorney General in refusing the requested leave must be

---

76 *Citizens Utilities Co. of California v. Superior Court for Alameda County*, 56 Cal. App. 3d 399, 404-406 (1976). The California attorney general recognizes this principle. See discussion and Attorney General Opinions cited on attorney general's web page, Opinion Unit, Quo Warranto Applications, Nature of the Remedy, Internet http://caag.state.ca.us/.

77 197 Cal. App. 2d 640 (1961).

extreme and clearly indefensible,"[78] but left no doubt that judicial intervention was indeed possible. "While the Attorney General argues that a court should never compel him to grant leave to sue in quo warranto, we need not make so sweeping a ruling." [79] The case involved a dispute between two cities over annexed territory.

In *Oakland Municipal Improvement League v. City of Oakland,*[80] in which citizen and union groups attacked a city charter reform for irregularity in enactment, the court noted that the line of reasonable discretion could be crossed:

> But if the Attorney General were to act in any case in an arbitrary way, denying without good cause a well-founded case presented by relators, it may be that he could be compelled by writ of mandate to proceed in the name of the people. It has not flatly been held but only suggested in these cases that this might be done, but it would be preferable so to hold outright if it were necessary, rather, than to declare the established rules of quo warranto, with the assurance they bring about ratified charters, to be unconstitutional. [Citations omitted]

And in *International Association of Firefighters, Local 55, AFL-CIO v. City of Oakland,*[81] where a union again challenged a charter amendment, the court remarked:

> And in a proper case where the proposed relator has an individual right distinct in kind from the right of the general public enforceable by an action in the nature of quo warranto, and where he has presented a proper petition with facts necessary to establish that right, we would not hesitate to hold that mandamus would issue to correct any arbitrary, capricious, or unreasonable action by the Attorney General in his control of such action.[82]

The Attorney General's office itself has affirmed that it has a duty to invoke the charter revocation procedure:

> It is the proper duty of the Attorney General to preserve to all the public the rights to which they are entitled by the

---

78 Id. at 648-650.
79 Id.
80 23 Cal. App. 3d 165, 172 (1972).
81 174 Cal. App. 3d 687 (1985).
82 Id. at 697.

> laws of the State of California and where it appears [the law has been violated] it is the duty of the Attorney General to properly present the matter before the courts of this state for a determination as to whether [there is] in fact a violation of the laws of the State of California.[83]

In approaching this duty, the attorney general's Opinion Unit has been applying a two-step analysis: "[W]e consider initially whether there exists a substantial question of law or fact that requires judicial resolution . . . ."[84] The present complaint on Unocal, of course, presents substantial questions of law and fact, to wit, whether the company is usurping or unlawfully exercising its authority, questions that can only be judicially determined. The attorney general's analysis then takes a second step, asking: "whether the proposed action would serve the overall public interest."[85] The Opinion Unit takes its guidance on "overall public interest" from *People v. Milk Producers Assn.*, 60 Cal.App. 439 (1923) at 444:

> "We think that, as has been indicated in some of the cases, the attorney general has some discretion in passing on complaints of public wrong (*Lamb v. Webb*, 151 Cal. 451); that he ought not to sue where the reasons urged for the beginning of an action in quo warranto are trivial or the purpose is to redress some grievance which is altogether private . . . ."

No reader of this complaint against Unocal will surmise that its reasons are trivial or private.

In sum, while the power to initiate corporate charter revocation proceedings is vested in the attorney general as the state's highest prosecutor, he or she must act responsibly, and the California courts maintain the right of judicial review of the decision to protect the interest of the people against both corporate abuses and arbitrary state power. It must be observed that none of the California cases cited above in which the courts ultimately refused to compel the attorney general to act involved allegations of harm and clear evidence of wrongdoing on a scale approaching that of the evidence offered to the attorney general in this present petition on Unocal. Moreover, the courts in every

---

83 22 Ops. Cal. Atty. Gen. 113, 121 (1953).
84 81 Ops. Cal. Atty. Gen. 98-100, 98-201, 98-208 (1998).
85 Id.

HEED 8/98

case gave close scrutiny to the attorney general's weighing of the evidence "in good conscience." It is clear he also owes the petitioners such a "good conscience" weighing and public analysis with respect to this Unocal petition.

Petitioners are not asking the attorney general for "leave to sue" Unocal themselves as "relators" on behalf on the People.

That procedure is authorized under the attorney general's administrative regulations,[86] but petitioners decline to invoke it at this time. We, instead, are petitioning the attorney general himself to act, as *Code of Civil Procedure* § 803 says he "must . . . whenever he has reason to believe" that a corporation has "usurped," or "unlawfully exercised" a corporate franchise. He acts under that statute on his own, at the directive of the governor, or "upon a complaint of a private party." This petition is such a complaint. Petitioners are declining to sue as "relators" because that mechanism is appropriate when the private party has some interest particular to him or her, in which the state and general public have little at stake, yet the attorney general's permission is needed before the private party can pursue justice.[87] The reason the attorney general's permission is needed at all for pursuit of private interests via *quo warranto* is an historical one dating from the Statute of Anne in 1710.[88] Here, petitioners are not seeking remedy of harms unique to them, but of harms to the public interest at large. It is legally the attorney general's duty to protect that interest. More importantly, only the full resources of the state will be adequate to challenge a corporation of Unocal's wealth and size. If the state were to tell petitioners that they may sue Unocal directly themselves, and that they must post a bond before doing so and guarantee they will pay "all costs and expenses incurred" in the litigation,[89] that would be a cynical message that the attorney general, abdicating his responsibility to protect the public, will nevertheless allow them to go into the lion's den themselves, armed with sticks.

---

86 11 *California Administrative Code* §§ 1-11.
87 81 Ops. Cal.Atty. Gen. 98-208 (1998).
88 *See* Chester J. Antieau, *The Practice of Extraordinary Remedies* §§ 4.00 et. seq. (1987), and discussion in *International Association of Firefighters, Local 55, AFL-CIO v. City of Oakland*, 174 Cal.App. 3d 687 (1985).
89 11 *California Administrative Code* § 6.

HEED 8/98

V. THE EVIDENCE AGAINST UNOCAL

The attorney general "must" initiate charter revocation proceedings when he has "reason to believe" that "any [corporate] franchise has been usurped, intruded into, or unlawfully exercised. . . ." *California Code of Civil Procedure § 803* . What would give the attorney general "reason to believe" would be:

- Evidence of acts either "perverting" the corporation's charter from its intended purposes or "usurping" authority not granted. *The People ex rel. Attorney General v. the Dashaway Association*, 84 Cal. 114, 119 (1890).

- Evidence that "the corporation has seriously offended against any provision of the statutes regulating corporations." *California Corporations Code §1801 (a) (1).*

- Evidence that it has "fraudulently abused or usurped corporate privileges or powers." *California Corporations Code §1801 (a) (2).*

The reference in §1801 (a) (1) to "the statutes regulating corporations" embraces not only laws imposing specific duties but also broad provisions such as the Unfair Competition Act, *California Business & Professions Code §§17200 et seq.,* and California's natural resources policy statutes, *California Government Code §§12600 et seq.*

The Unfair Competition Act prohibits "any unlawful, unfair or fraudulent business act or practice." *Id. at §17200.* That phrase incorporates "any practices forbidden by law, be it civil, criminal, federal, state, or municipal, statutory, regulatory, or court-made."[90] "[A]n 'unfair' business practice occurs when it offends an established public policy or when the practice is immoral, unethical, oppressive, unscrupulous or substantially injurious to consumers."[91] The statute incorporates international law since "[f]rom the earliest days of this republic

---

90 *Saunders v. Superior Court,* 27 Cal. App. 4th 832, 839 (1994).
91 *The People v. Casa Blanca Convalescent Homes* 159 Cal. app. 3d 509, 530 (1984).

1   our international obligations have been considered part of controlling
common law."[92] <u>Thus, violations of international law that take place</u>
2   <u>thousands of miles overseas by California corporations are also viola-</u>
3   <u>tions of California law, actionable here. This is not theory, but hard</u>
<u>California law.</u>
4   California's natural resources policy statutes, *California Gov-*
5   *ernment Code §§12600 et seq.*, declare that it is "the policy of this
state to conserve, protect, and enhance its environment . . . [and] to
6   prevent destruction, pollution, or irreparable impairment of the envi-
7   ronment and the natural resources of this state." *Id.* at §12600 (a). The
attorney general has authority to bring actions for equitable relief to
8   protect the policy. *Id.* at §12607.
9   Petitioners believe the evidence adduced below on information
10 and belief shows that through many years of destructive activities Union
Oil Company of California ("Unocal") has committed many acts con-
11 stituting "perversion" of its charter, "usurpation" of authority not
12 granted, "serious offense against the statutes regulating corporations,"
and "fraudulent abuse of corporate powers and privileges." Petition-
13 ers believe there can be no question that the attorney general has ample
14 "reason to believe" that the company should be the target of a charter
15 revocation proceeding.

16   **Clarifying the legal entity that is the subject of this complaint.**
17   Union Oil Company of California is one of California's oldest
corporations, incorporated in this state in 1890. Although a "Unocal
18 Corporation" was incorporated in Delaware in 1983 and technically
19 became the parent company, the Delaware entity is a mere paper corporation. The principal officers of Unocal and Union Oil Company of
20 California are the same persons with different titles, and both entities
21 are headquartered in the same offices at 2141 Rosecrans Avenue, Suite
4000, El Segundo, California 90245. A "legal note" inside the front
22 cover of the 1997 Annual Report explains: "Unocal Corporation is the
23 parent of Union Oil Company of California. Virtually all operations
are conducted by Union Oil Company of California, which does busi-
24 ness as Unocal, and its subsidiaries."
25   Thus, while referring throughout to "Unocal," this petition seeks
26 to revoke the charter of Union Oil Company of California, the entity

27 ——————

28 92 *People v. Ghent*, 43 Cal. 3d 739, 780 (1987) (Mosk concurring opinion).

actually conducting the operations and the one with which the state of California has an historic relationship and over which the state has concomitant authority. Should it become necessary at a later date, petitioners will also file a petition in Delaware to dissolve "Unocal Corporation."

Union Oil Company's charter.

The company's California charter is its articles of incorporation, amended in recent years to take advantage of the state's liberalized *Corporations Code* § 202, allowing corporations to engage "in any lawful act or activity for which a corporation may be organized." The *Corporations Code* is a typical "general incorporation statute" that replaced the former company-by-company charters during the infamous "race to the bottom" recounted in an earlier section of this petition. But while it allows any corporation to incorporate merely by filing its "articles of incorporation" with the Secretary of State instead of applying to the legislature for a charter, the *Corporations Code* does not overturn the earlier California case law or the quo warranto statutes requiring corporations to stick within their charters. Admittedly, these charters, that is, their articles of incorporation, are now broad boilerplates, but they do contain these limits: corporate activity must be (1) "lawful," (2) something for which a for-profit business may be organized, and (3) always in accord with the public policy of the state. The first of these limits is found in the language of Code § 202 and the corporations' articles. The second derives from the fact that this section of the Code is authorizing for-profit business enterprises and not, e.g., charitable, religious, social, governmental or political ones. The third limit is inherent in the common law doctrine of California that the law may never be construed to authorize violations of public policy.

Petitioners believe on the basis of the information referenced below that over the years Unocal has strayed far from this authorized path, violating local, state, federal and international law, acting unethically, contravening public policy, usurping political power, and causing great harm to the people of California and the world. Petitioners believe the evidence shows Unocal to be a repeat offender, with international operations and a net worth in the billions of dollars, operating globally with virtual impunity, occasionally paying fines for its harms as a cost of doing business, while often passing onto society the true costs of its operations. Unocal recently announced that it "no longer considers itself as a U.S. company," but as "a global energy company."[93] Since Unocal has let go of the U.S., petitioners believe it is time for the U.S. to let go of Unocal, while making certain that its assets remain available to compensate for harms it may have done. The State of California, which granted the Union Oil Company of California existence, possesses the greatest responsibility to protect the public from the goliath it created. It is incumbent upon the attorney general, who has sworn to be tough on crime, to initiate proceedings to dissolve the corporation.

Preserving Unocal's assets, assuring justice and equity.

As part of the attorney general's initial action, we request that he apply to the court also to "appoint a receiver to take over and manage the business and affairs of the corporation and to preserve its property pending the hearing and determination of the complaint for dissolution," in the words of *California Corporations Code* § 1803. We also request that the Attorney General ask the court to exercise its authority under *Corporations Code* § 1804 in winding up the company to "make such orders and decrees and issue such injunctions in the case as justice and equity require," in order to fully protect jobs, workers, stockholders, unions, communities, the environment, suppliers, customers, governmental entities, and the public interest. Petitioners stand ready to participate in an advisory committee to assist the attorney general in formulating such proposed orders to assure a smooth transformation of Unocal into an economic entity or entities that will be law abiding, socially just, humane, and ecologically sustainable.

---

93   "Unocal Becomes A Company Without A Nation," 12 *Business Ethics* 6 (January/February 1998).

HEED 8/98

Count 1. Ecocide: Environmental Devastation

On the basis of the information stated and footnoted below, petitioners believe there is strong reason for the attorney general to find the following to be true:

As an oil and gas company, Unocal deals with a product that is inherently dangerous to the environment: dangerous to extract, dangerous to transport to market, dangerous to consume.[94] The company cannot be faulted for going into the business in 1890 that has principally fueled the economy of the entire Twentieth century. But, knowing that it was in an unusually dangerous business, Unocal owed the public a duty of care.

In this it has failed. Its record is one of reckless pursuit of profits and insensitivity toward its duty of care. If California's "three-strikes you're out" legislation were applicable to corporate environmental violations, Unocal, a recidivist polluter, would have long since been out of business. In addition to the instances selected below for illustration, Unocal has compiled a long list of environmental liabilities over the years. In its Annual Report for 1997, for instance, speaking only of "Superfund and similar sites," the company discloses:

> At year end 1997, Unocal had received notification from the U.S. Environmental Protection Agency that the company may be a potentially responsible party (PRP) at 41 sites . . . . In addition, various state agencies and private parties had identified 41 other similar PRP sites . . . . of the total, the company has denied responsibility at six sites . . . . These 82 sites exclude 60 sites where the company's liability has been settled, or where the company has no evidence

---

94 The California Air Resources Board tallies emissions of four health-damaging pollutants: reactive organic gases (ROG), nitrogen oxides (Nox), sulfur oxides (Sox), and particulate matter (PM). Emissions of these gases by oil and gas producers at the wellsite and the refinery rival the air pollution created by all forms of industrial manufacturing combined. One example of toxic pollution created by the refining process is dioxin, created in the process of refining petroleum. "One in ten children suffer from slow learning as a result of dioxin exposure," according to Greg Karras, senior scientist at Communities for a Better Environment. "Yet major known dioxin polluters, including oil refineries, still cover up the amounts of their ongoing dioxin release." California Public Interest Research Group (CALPIRG), *Crude Policy, Subsidies of the Oil Industry by California Taxpayers* 3 (December 1997).

of liability and there has been no further indication of liability by government agencies or third parties for at least a 12 month period. Unocal does not consider the number of sites for which it has been named a PRP as a relevant measure of liability . . . .[95]

The company's environmental devastation extends from local to global and is serious enough to describe as ecocide.[96] The following handful of examples are an illustrative, not exhaustive, list of Unocal's harms to the environment:

---

95 Unocal Corp., *Annual Report 1997* (1998).
96 Mark Alan Gray, legal scholar and First Secretary of the Australian Permanent Mission to the United Nations, argues convincingly that a norm has now emerged within customary international law imposing a duty of care owed to humanity in general to avoid massive harm to the natural environment. He calls breach of the duty "ecocide," identifiable as harm that involves "(1) serious, and extensive or lasting, ecological damage, (2) international consequences, and (3) waste . . . [i.e.] when there are social benefits they are greatly outweighed by social costs." See Mark Alan Gray, "The International Crime of Ecocide," *26 California Western International Law Journal* 215 (1996). The norm is expressed in multiple sources which, together, constitute evidence of its obligatory nature as a matter of international law: the tort law, statutory law and doctrinal law of nations; judicial decisons in international law; treaties; declarations and resolutions of international bodies. Within these sources, particularly salient expressions of the norm are implicit in doctrines of nuisance, negligence, public trust, and *sic utere tuo ut alienum non laedas* ; treaties such as the U.N. Framework Convention on Climate Change (31 I.L.M. 849), International Convention on Civil Liability for Oil Pollution Damage (973 U.N.T.,S. 3, 9 I.L.M. 45), United Nations Convention on the Law of the Sea (21 I.L.M. 1261), Vienna Convention for the Protection of the Ozone Layer (26 I.L.M. 1529), Geneva Convention on Long-Range Transboundary Air Pollution (18 I.L.M. 1442), Convention on Biological Diversity (31 I.L.M. 818), Basel Convention on the Control of Transboundary Movements of Hazardous Wastes and Their Disposal (28 I.L.M. 657), Universal Declaration of Human Rights (G.A. Res. 217 (III), U.N. Doc. A/810 (1948)) , International Covenant on Civil and Political Rights (999 U.N.T.S. 171, 6 I.L.M. 368), and the International Covenant on Economic, Social and Cultural Rights (993 U.N.T.S. 3, 6 I.L.M. 360); and documents such as the Stockholm Declaration (11 I.L.M. 1416), Rio Declaration (31 I.L.M. 874), Agenda 21 (Report of the United Nations Conference on Environment and Development, U.N. Doc. A/CONF. 151/26 (Vol. 1) (1992)), the World Charter for Nature (G.A. Res. 7, U.N. GAOR, 37th Sess., Supp. No. 51, U.N. Doc. A/Res./37/7 (1982)) and the Draft Code of Crimes Against the Peace and Security of Mankind ((1991) 2(II)Y.B. International Law Commission 94-97).

California.

Unocal has demonstrated a pattern and practice of polluting the locations where it operates. The company was the primary operator in the notorious Santa Barbara Channel oil blowout of 1969 which shocked Californians and woke the nation to the need to restrict oil drilling in coastal waters. Company President Fred Hartley told a U.S. Senate hearing at the time that he was "amazed at the publicity for the loss of a few birds."[97] Thirty years later, Unocal has proven itself an incorrigible recidivist environmental polluter.

• **Guadalupe: biggest spill in U.S. history?** Portions of an 18-mile stretch of coastline between San Luis Obispo and Santa Barbara County, part of it a registered National Landmark, are contaminated with diluent, a kerosene-like substance that has been leaking for years from Unocal's operations in the Guadalupe oil field. County officials estimate the spill at between 8 and 20 million gallons; the Surfers' Environmental Alliance puts it at 50 million, making it "the biggest eco-disaster in U.S. history."[98] The mostly Latino residents of the nearby farming town of Guadalupe depend upon the local water source for drinking and many also fish nearby for food. Recent tests show the fish are contaminated by the spill.[99] The Surfers' Environmental Alliance has sued, as has the California Attorney General, the latter claiming unlawful discharge into marine and state waters, failure to report discharges, destruction of natural resources, failure to warn and exposure to known carcinogens, public nuisance, unauthorized disposal of hazardous waste, and labeling violations for "recycled" diluent. The Attorney General is acting on behalf of the Department of Fish and Game, the Regional Water Quality Control Board and the Department of Toxic Substances Control.[100] It was announced on July 22, 1998, that the Attorney General settled the action when Unocal agreed to pay $43.8 million, perhaps the largest amount in such a case in Cali-

---

97 *New York Times*, February 6, 1969 at 19 (New York Times Information Bank Abstracts).

98 "Surfers' Environmental Alliance," *City News Service*, Los Angeles, March 10, 1998; John D. Cox, "Once-Popular Avila Beach Goes From Tourists to Toxic," *Sacramento Bee*, September 8, 1997 at A1.

99 "Surfers' Environmental Alliance," supra note 242.

100 Unocal Corporation, Annual Report Securities Exchange Commission Form 10-K (March 1998), available at Internet site http://sec.yahoo.com/e/980331/ucl.html.

fornia history — as appropriate for the largest spill.[101] The amount does not include costs of cleanup.

• **Avila Beach: killing a town's economy.** Unocal began operating in Avila Beach, a popular tourist town in San Luis Obispo County, in 1906. The company installed pipelines underneath the main street ("Front Street") to connect its storage tanks to the "Unocal pier" at the beach. By 1989 it was discovered that crude oil and refined products had been leaking for years from the pipes into the ground under Front Street and the beach, contaminating a huge area of soil and groundwater. Regional authorities eventually issued a Cleanup and Abatement Order. Unocal's response was to appeal, sue the authorities and fight their plan. In 1995, an excavation of the town became necessary when petroleum hydrocarbons under the sand were discovered at a depth of only two and one half feet from daylight. Tourism has disappeared, economically the town is dead. Unocal has now entered cleanup negotiations and CEO Roger Beach has publicly apologized to the citizens of Avila Beach, promising "to regain their trust." But massive litigation has resulted, with the State Attorney General and the County filing notices of intent to sue, and numerous Avila businesses, individuals and organizations filing suits for multiple violations, including allegations that Unocal has not been accurate and truthful and has concealed from the public and government the true extent of the contamination.[102] The company recently agreed to a cleanup plan that may cost it up to $200 million.[103]

• **San Francisco Bay: running a hazardous Rodeo.** Unocal ran a repeatedly hazardous refinery at the town of Rodeo until it sold it to

---

101 "Unocal OKs $43.8 Million Settlement," *San Francisco Chronicle*, July 22, 1998 at A24.

102 Unocal Corporation, Annual Report Securities Exchange Commission Form 10-K (March 1998), available at Internet site http://sec.yahoo.com/e/980331/ucl.html; Avila Alliance et al. v. Unocal Corporation et al., Superior Court for San Luis Obispo County, State of California (No. CV 079728), Second Amended Complaint (filed May 7, 1997); Unocal web site at www.unocal.com/. . ./96hesrpt/hestrust.htm; John D. Cox, "Once-Popular Avila Beach Goes From Tourists to Toxic," *Sacramento Bee*, September 8, 1997 at A1.

103 "Unocal Agrees to Massive Cleanup of Avila Beach; Environment," *Los Angeles Times,* June 18, 1998 at A-1.

Tosco Corporation in 1997. Numerous charges against Unocal by the Bay Area Air Quality Air Management District were recently resolved with a $280,000 payment.[104] In 1994, the refinery leaked catacarb, an odorless, hazardous chemical, for 16 days with the knowledge of plant managers who told health officials, workers and the public that it was harmless. More than 700 workers and thousands of nearby residents were exposed, many of whom reported falling ill from the chemical. The company paid $3 million in criminal and civil fines to Contra Costa County in 1995 for the discharge and in 1997 agreed to pay $80 million to settle private lawsuits for 18,000 individuals as well as a $375,000 penalty to the federal Environmental Protection Agency.[105] In 1997 the company lost a law suit brought by environmental groups under the federal Clean Water Act and California's Unfair Competition Act for dumping selenium in San Francisco Bay. In high concentrations, selenium can cause birth defects, deformities, and death. "Unocal's pollution stemmed from its decision to buy less costly but selenium-rich crude oil for its Rodeo refinery, according to environmentalists. . . . The Bay became contaminated, leading health officials to warn people not to eat some Bay area fish and shellfish. . . . 'Poor people rely on fishing in the Bay for food,' says environmentalist Karras. 'Eighty percent of them are people of color. This is a form of environmental racism.'"[106] The court found Unocal had violated federal laws almost daily. Liability could exceed $50 million.[107]

• **Mountain Pass: keeping toxic spills quiet.** The San Bernardino County district attorney is conducting a criminal investigation and has filed a civil suit and over Unocal's pollution of ground water and failure to inform the public of toxic discharges at its Molycorp Mountain Pass Mine which is less than one mile from an elementary school. Molycorp, a Unocal subsidiary, "allegedly acted too late to inform workers and residents of its toxic discharges. The company

---

104 Michael Hytha, "Final Unocal Payment for Pollution," *San Francisco Chronicle*, July 7, 1998 at A15.
105 Michael Hytha, "Study Blames Illness on Unocal Leak," *San Francisco Chronicle*, August 21, 1997 at A17; "EPA Fines Unocal For '94 Toxic Release," *San Francisco Chronicle*, May 9, 1997, at A23.
106 Reese Erlich, "Burma-Business: Oil Giant Suffers Legal Setbacks," *Inter Press Service*, May 8, 1997.
107 "Unocal Guilty of Dumping a Chemical Into San Francisco Bay," *New York Times*, April 20, 1997, at I-23.

HEED 8/98

sent a letter to residents . . . after it learned it was a target for a Proposition 65 lawsuit."[108] Some 350,000 gallons of toxic wastewater gushed from pipeline breaks in 1996 and is still polluting ground water. Molycorp is being pursued by the federal Bureau of Land Management, County Fire Department, and the Regional Water Quality Control Board which fined the company $550,000, the highest figure in its history, for violating requirements to report discharges. Unocal is fighting the penalty.[109]

- **Los Angeles: buying the right to pollute low-income Latino neighborhoods.** Communities for a Better Environment (CBE) has sued Unocal and its successor Tosco under the federal Clean Air Act for failing to install vapor recovery equipment at their harbor terminal where they load oil tanker ships. The suit alleges: The predominantly low-income Latino communities nearby are disproportionately affected by the health risks resulting from the hundreds of pounds of chemical vapors released every time an oil tanker is loaded. Marine vapor recovery equipment has been shown effective and has been installed at most facilities in Los Angeles and nationwide—and even by Unocal in San Francisco. But in Los Angeles, Unocal and two other companies chose instead to lobby the Southern California Air Quality Management District to adopt a loophole rule allowing the companies to buy and scrap old cars, on the theory that the action would remove about the same amount of pollution as the marine vapor equipment. There are two problems with the theory. First, even if it worked, the company would be committing an act of environmental racism because cleaner air for the region would be achieved at the cost of continued unhealthy air for low-income Latinos. Second, the theory does not work: the evidence shows that many of the cars scrapped were not driven anyway, some are actually put back on the road, and many would have been destroyed by natural attrition; so the clean air gains boasted by the program are an illusion. The federal EPA has formally rejected the car scrapping rule as a violation of the federal Clean Air Act. Unocal is violating the Act, as well as the California Unfair Competition Act,

---

108 Jack McCarthy, "Mine Company Sued Over Tainted Water," *The Press Enterprise*, May 20, 1998.

109 Id. Unocal Corporation, Annual Report Securities Exchange Commission Form 10-K (March 1998), available at Internet site http://sec.yahoo.com/e/980331/ucl.html.

but is fighting the case in court.[110]

These violations in California alone work a forfeiture of Unocal's corporate charter because the charter has been "unlawfully exercised,"[111] and "perverted,"[112] in "serious offen[se]" against "the statutes regulating corporations,"[113] including the Unfair Competition Act which prohibits "any unlawful, unfair or fraudulent business act or practice"[114] and California's natural resources policy statutes, *California Government Code* §§12600 *et seq.*, which declare that it is "the policy of this state to conserve, protect, and enhance its environment. . . [and] to prevent destruction, pollution, or irreparable impairment of the environment and the natural resources of this state." *Id.* at § 12600 (a).

Changing the climate.

Along with other oil and gas companies, Unocal is a primary producer of the fossil fuels that release greenhouse gases and are changing the global climate, resulting in an environmental crisis that could become the worst ever faced by humankind. "The avoidance of climate catastrophe requires a rapid phase-out of fossil fuels—especially oil and coal—and a transition to safe and renewable forms of energy."[115] Some oil companies acknowledge the threat, recognize their role in it, and claim that they have begun to think about the necessary transition out of the fossil fuel era. John Browne, group chief executive of the British Petroleum company, delivered a major address at Stanford University in 1997 in which he said:

> There is now an effective consensus among the world's leading scientists and serious and well-informed people outside the scientific community that there is a discernible human influence on the climate and a link between the concentration of carbon dioxide and the increase in temperature. We must now focus on what can and what should be done, not

---

110 *Communities for a Better Environment v. Unocal et al* (U.S. Dist. Court Central Dist. of Cal., Civil No. 97-5414 DT (BQRx), January 21, 1998).
111 California Code of Civil Procedure § 803.
112 *Dashaway*, supra note 69.
113 California Corporations Code § 1801 (a) (1).
114 California Business & Professions Code § 17200.
115 "Oilwatch/NGO Declaration on Climate Change, Fossil Fuels and Public Funding," signed by nearly 200 environmental organizations on five continents (Kyoto, December 2, 1997).

because we can be certain climate change is happening but because the possibility can't be ignored. If we are all to take responsibility for the future of our planet, then it falls to us to begin to take precautionary action now.[116]

Some other oil companies have followed suit.[117] Whether this is merely another "toxic greenwash,"[118] more corporate PR, remains to be seen. But Unocal has not even risen to this new level of concessionary rhetoric. It has funded a researcher to throw doubt on the climate change science[119] while it charges ahead touting its "new exploration blocks," "new proven reserves," and "expect[ed] average 6 to 8 percent growth in our worldwide production through the year 2001." [120] This company is the largest geothermal developer in the world.[121] Geothermal can sometimes be harmful to local environments, but it is not a greenhouse gas emitter. Yet Unocal is not using its geothermal path as a way out of the fossil fuel business.

In their intentional disregard for the consequences of their product, oil companies behaving like Unocal are breaching a duty of care owed under ordinary tort law just as tobacco companies have done. No one has yet challenged them. They are breaching the standard of care set by the Climate Change Convention[122] and the Kyoto Protocol,[123] treaties which establish the international regulatory framework for nations, but which may also be used to measure the standard of care required by private parties. They are violating the international human right to a clean and healthy environment[124] and are committing

---

116 James Gerstenzang, "Oil Executive Breaks With Industry," *Los Angeles Times*, May 21, 1997 at A-3.

117 Martha M. Hamilton, "Global Warming Gets a 2nd Look; Oil Executives Are Shifting Their Stance," *The Washington Post*, March 3, 1998 at C01.

118 Joshua Karliner, *The Corporate Planet* ch. 6, (1998).

119 Jean Dubail, "Global Warming; Best Scientific Minds Agree: The Need To Act Is Clear," *Cleveland Plain Dealer*, December 15, 1997 at 9B.

120 Unocal Corporation, Annual Report 1997, at 6 (1998).

121 Unocal Corp., Annual Report 1997 (1998).

122 31 I.L.M. 849.

123 B.N.A., "Kyoto Protocol to the UN Framework Convention on Climate Change," *21 International Environment Reporter* 3901, 3951.

124 Janusz Symonides, "The Human Right to a Clean, Balanced and Protected Environment," *20 International Journal of Legal Information* 24 (1992).

1 | ecocide. The fact that no one has yet asserted a tort or international law remedy against the oil companies should encourage rather than
2 | deter the attorney general in asserting the independent charter revoca-
3 | tion remedy, especially when, as with Unocal, the company has been entailed in a host of other environmental violations. The attorney gen-
4 | eral may move to revoke Unocal's charter for these international law
5 | violations under *California Business and Professions Code* § 17200 which prohibits any "unlawful" business practice including interna-
6 | tional ones. That section, in turn, provides the basis for charter revo-
7 | cation under *California Code of Civil Procedure* § 803, and *Corpora-*
8 | *tions Code* § 1801.

9 | **Burma pipeline in rainforest region.**
10 | Of all places where fossil fuel production must be phased out first, rainforest zones are at the top of the list because intrusion there carries
11 | the double threat of both biodiversity loss and climate change. The
12 | Kyoto Declaration by nearly 200 environmental groups on five conti- nents calls for a moritorium on new fossil fuel exploration in "pristine
13 | and frontier areas."[125] Unocal's activities in Burma, described fully
14 | below in Counts Five to Seven, have permanently altered the pipeline
15 | region. Unocal says the 39-mile on-land route of the pipeline was cho- sen to minimize the environmental impact. "By making a significant
16 | detour, the route goes mainly through thinly wooded terrain except for
17 | a few kilometres through primary tropical moist forest."[126] Not men- tioned is that the Tenasserim region which the pipeline traverses pos-
18 | sesses the largest block of intact rainforest in Southeast Asia, accord-
19 | ing to the World Wildlife Fund.[127] "Indo-Burma" has been added as one of Conservation International's twenty-four "hotspots" of global
20 | biodiversity, notable for both tremendous biological diversity and a
21 | very high degree of threat.[128] It possesses 7,000 separate plant species which are found nowhere else.[129] After the pipeline reaches Thailand
22 | (where Unocal does not control it) it will plunge through pristine ar-
23 |
24 |
25 | 125 "Oilwatch/NGO Declaration on Climate Change, Fossil Fuels and Pub- lic Funding," signed by nearly 200 environmental organizations on five
26 | continents (Kyoto, Dec. 2, 1997).
127 | 126 Total, *The Yadana Gas Development Project* 5 (1997).
127 | 127 World Wildlife Fund, *Global 200 Ecoregions* (Draft, August 1997).
128 | 128 Conservation International, "Annual Report 1997" (1998).
28 | 129 Id.

eas including national parks and world heritage sites.[130] Unocal's position ignores the damage to rainforests done by access roads and infrastructure. It also ignores the impact on precious natural sites in Thailand after the pipeline leaves Unocal's hands. In these ways, Unocal is violating its legal duty of care to the environment under international law.

The offshore portion of the pipeline in the Andaman Sea also puts the environment at risk. Gas exploration and production produces large quantities of toxic wastes and atmospheric emissions. In the United States the operations would be heavily regulated, but not in Burma.[131]

No independent Environmental Impact Assessments of the project have been conducted or subjected to public scrutiny.[132]

On these facts, the Attorney General has good reason to believe that Unocal is breaching the standard of care set by the Convention on Biological Diversity,[133] breaching the international right to a clean and healthy environment (which includes rights to information and participation in environmental impact assessment) and is committing ecocide. The Attorney General may move to revoke Unocal's charter for these violations via *California Business and Professions Code* § 17200, *Code of Civil Procedure* § 803 and *Corporations Code* § 1801, as described above.

---

130 Danielle Knight, "Environment: U.S. Greens Join Protest Against Thai Pipeline," *Inter Press Service*, February 23,1998.
131 Earth Rights International (ERI) and Southeast Asia Information Network (SAIN), *Total Denial: A Report on the Yadana Pipeline Project In Burma* 54-55 (1996).
132 Id. at 55.
133 31 I.L.M. 818.

HEED 8/98

Count 2. Unfair and Unethical Treatment of Workers

On the basis of the information stated and footnoted below, petitioners believe there is strong reason for the Attorney General to find the following to be true:

When Unocal declared that "it no longer considers itself as a U.S. company," but rather as "a global energy company,"[134] it made no effort to hide its strategy of selling off its American refineries and gasoline stations in order to finance expanding oil and gas production overseas.[135] This move took the value that generations of its American workers had helped to build, abandoned those and future generations of American workers as if they were disposable cogs in a profit-making machine, and moved into repressive countries where the company could exploit cheap and even slave foreign labor. While this is an increasingly typical story as U.S. companies move offshore abetted by free trade agreements and cheered on by extremist economic ideologues,[136] it is not an ethical story, nor one that the People of the State of California, represented by the attorney general, must sit cross-legged listening to.

When the California Legislature in the *Corporations Code* authorized the corporate form of doing business "for any lawful act or activity,"[137] it did not simultaneously authorize Unocal's kind of slash-and-burn capitalism. It is implicit in the statute, as in every statute, that the persons subject to it will act ethically and in good faith. Obedience to the standards of the regulatory state—wage and hour standards, health and safety rules, non-discrimination, rights to organize unions, etc.—does not exhaust the duties of corporations to the public and their workers.

The very existence of corporations is permitted only against the background of fear of "the slavery that would result from aggregations of capital in the hands of a few individuals and corporations," noted by the U.S. Supreme Court when it approved the revocation of Standard Oil's corporate charter, [138] and the "fear of the subjection of

---

134 "Unocal Becomes a Company Without a Nation," *12 Business Ethics*, 6 (January/February 1998)
135 Unocal Corporation, *1997 Annual Report* 6 (1998).
136 Robert W. Benson, "Free Trade As An Extremist Ideology: The Case of NAFTA," *17 University of Puget Sound Law Review* 149 (1994).
137 California Corporations Code § 202(b)(1)
138 *Standard Oil of New Jersey v. United States,* 221 U.S. 1 at 83 (1911).

1 labor to capital" by a corporate "feudal" "plutocracy" noted by Justice
Brandeis two generations ago.[139] Given this background, the Legisla-
2 ture that enacted the *Corporations Code* surely must have intended
3 that corporations act ethically and in good faith to be permitted to
exist.
4
Moreover, the Unfair Competition Act prohibits any "unfair or
5 fraudulent business act or practice,"[140] and "an 'unfair' business practice occurs when it offends an established public policy or when the
6 practice is immoral, unethical, oppressive, unscrupulous or substan-
7 tially injurious to consumers,"[141] a description which fits Unocal's la-
8 bor practices to a T. "California courts have recognized that an
employer's business practices concerning its employees are within the
9 scope of section §17200."[142]
10 Among Unocal's practices that violate the *Corporations Code* and
the Unfair Competition Act are the following:
11

12 **Discarding workers to make a sale.**
Obviously corporations must sometimes lay off workers, but ethi-
13 cally the workers must be treated in good faith with the dignity due
14 human beings and not suddenly pushed out the door in order to raise
investment cash, or sold out to hardball, union-busting companies bent
15 on slashing employee ranks. In 1996, Uno-Ven, a company half-owned
16 by Unocal, locked out 450 members of the Oil, Chemical and Atomic
17 Workers International Union (OCAW) in Lemont, Illinois, in a brutal
attempt to extract concessions and raise capital for investment over-
18 seas. Nine months later, days after the lockout ended, Unocal announced
19 it was selling its share and, according to press reports, taking the capital to places abroad where employees have few rights. Months after
20 the lockout many workers lost jobs when another concessionary con-
21 tract was forced on them.[143]
In 1997, Unocal sold all its U.S. refinery and marketing opera-
22

23 ─────────────
139 *Liggett Co. v. Lee*, 288 U.S. 517, 548, 565 (1933) (Brandeis dissent).
24 140 California Business & Professions Code '17200.
141 *The People v. Casa Blanca Convalescent Homes*, 159 C.A.3d 509, 530
25 (1984).
142 *Application Group v. Hunter Group*, 61 Cal. App. 4th 881, 907 (1998).
26 143 David Johnson, "As CITGO Takes Over at Lemont, Labor Strife Loom-
27 ing," *Platt's Oilgram News*, May 23, 1997; "CITGO Takeover of Uno-
Ven Illinois Refinery Ruffles Workers," *Dow Jones Telerate Energy Ser-
28 vice*, May 20, 1997.

tions to Tosco Corporation, a company "known for its ability to squeeze profit out of refineries it has purchased and for its tough tactics in doing so. Last year, Tosco closed a refinery in Pennsylvania until the union there agreed to job cuts."[144]

> In all, almost 900 Unocal employees lost their jobs at refining and marketing operations. In the refineries, Unocal supervisors working with Tosco decided, even before the sale was complete, who would lose their livelihood in this latest downsizing. Many of the workers who lost jobs had 30 years of service and were in their 50's. The majority had participated in various 'long term' medical treatment programs—as a result of injuries sustained on the job. Seven had been diagnosed with cancer.[145]

Endangering workers' safety.

U.S. Occupational Safety and Health Administration records list hundreds of OSHA violations against Unocal from 1985 to 1997.[146] Unocal holds the record for the second worst oil disaster in U.S. history when 17 workers were killed in an explosion at its Romeoville, Illinois, plant in 1984.[147] Now, by selling out to cost-cutters and moving to Asia, it is leaving behind an even greater risk.

> The job cuts and switch to contract workers that often follow independent company takeovers of larger companies' refineries strain the refineries' ability to operate safely. At the California Unocal refinery sites that were taken over by Tosco, fewer workers will now be expected to do exactly the same amount of work as the former larger workforce. The layoffs also include workers in such critical safety areas as firefighting. The cuts and contracting out have been major contributing causes to the rash of plant explosions and safety incidents in the past decade. Between 1984 and 1991, fires and explosions at U.S. oil refineries and related

144 Nancy Rivera Brooks, "Union Says Tosco Threatened Closure," *Los Angeles Times*, March 26, 1997, at D-2.
145 Joseph J. Drexler, OCAW Special Projects Director, "Remarks to the International Indigenous People's Tribunal in Conjunction with The Other Economic Summit (TOES)," Denver, June 19, 1997.
146 Records available on OSHA Internet site www.osha.gov.
147 Kristina Markus, "Still Ringing in Their Ears," *Chicago Tribune*, August 3, 1994.

facilities killed more than 80 workers and injured 651 more.[148]

At a Tosco refinery near Martinez, California, a fire blazed through the plant in January of 1997, killing one worker. "The Tosco accident is only one of many in along line of explosions and fires that have killed and maimed our members, other workers and community residents in recent years," says Robert Wages, president of OCAW. "How many people are going to have to die before we do something to halt this madness?"[149]

Exploiting cheap and slave labor abroad.

Unocal's complicity in the use of forced labor by its military business partner in Burma will be fully described in Count Five, below, and is incorporated here by reference as if fully set forth. It must be added that Unocal's deal with the dictatorship helps the junta to brutally suppress all independent labor unions in that country and to imprison leading union leaders, creating labor conditions which redound to the benefit of foreign companies like Unocal. The Federation of Trade Unions of Burma, the independent labor association of Burma operating from exile offices in Thailand, is a plaintiff in one of two lawsuits filed against Unocal in Los Angeles.[150] The U.S. AFL-CIO has also condemned Unocal for its complicity in Burma:

> U.S. based oil companies. . . stubbornly continue to prop up the military regime by providing it with large amounts of desperately needed hard currency. In addition to Unocal, ARCO . . . [is] engaged in exploration that may provide SLORC with significant additional capital. This is occurring at the same time that oil companies are engaged in severe downsizing and cost-cutting which has compromised worker and community safety and is resulting in a significant loss of high-skill, high-wage jobs in the United States.[151]

---

148 Jenna E. Ziman, "The Social and Environmental Costs of Oil Company Divistment from U.S. Refineries," *Multinational Monitor,* May 1997, available on Internet site www.essential.org. See also, Jack Doyle, "Oil Slick: Profits Abroad and Poison at Home; Big Petroleum Ships Out, Leaving Behind a Big Mess," *Washington Post,* July 31, 1994.
149 Quoted in Ziman, supra note 148.
150 *National Coalition Government et al. v. Unocal,* infra note 250.
151 AFL-CIO Executive Council, "Burma," February 19, 1997.

Thus, Unocal is not a good-faith consumer of marketplace labor, but an aggressive, unscrupulous manipulator of that marketplace, unethically exploiting its U.S. workers, oppressing its foreign workers, and walking away with profits built on the backs of both.

The violations above work a forfeiture of Unocal's corporate charter because the charter has been "unlawfully exercised,"[152] and "perverted,"[153] in "serious offen[se]" against "the statutes regulating corporations,"[154] including the *Corporations Code*,[155] and the Unfair Competition Act prohibiting "any unlawful, unfair or fraudulent business act or practice."[156]

---

152 California Code of Civil Procedure § 803.
153 *Dashaway*, supra note 69.
154 California Corporations Code § 1801 (a) (1).
155 California Corporations Code § 202.
156 California Business and Professions Code § 17200.

HEED 8/98

Count 3. Complicity in Crimes Against Humanity:[157]
Aiding Oppression of Women

On the basis of the information stated and footnoted below, petitioners believe there is strong reason for the Attorney General to find the following to be true:

Unocal has initiated business dealings with a repressive rebel military force in Afghanistan infamous for gross violations of human rights. The company is lead partner, holding 54.11% in CentGas. "Unocal has been instrumental in forming the seven-member CentGas consortium for the future construction of a gas pipeline from Turkmenistan through Afghanistan to growing markets in Pakistan and, potentially, India . . . . Unocal hopes to form a similar consortium for an oil pipeline from the newly independent states of Central Asia through Afghanistan and Pakistan to the Arabian Sea"[158] To accomplish this, Unocal has opened negotiations with the Taliban, who are not a recognized government, but a militia faction of Muslim extremists in a nation at civil war. The Taliban's mission includes denying basic freedoms to females. As explained below, Unocal as business partner can be held liable under traditional U.S. and California law for the Taliban's violations of human rights.

On September 27, 1996, the Taliban overthrew the existing government and controlled 85% of Afghanistan.[159] "On 1 October [1996], Chris Taggart, executive vice-president of Unocal, told Reuters news agency, 'We regard it (the Taliban victory) as very positive.' He urged the US to extend recognition to the new rulers in Kabul and thus "lead

---

157 Crimes against humanity, first defined in the Nuremberg Charter as "inhumane acts committed against any civilian population" as a matter of government policy in wartime, are part of customary international criminal law imposing duties and liabilities upon individuals as well as states. See Nuremberg Charter (Agreement for the Prosecution and Punishment of the Major War Criminals of the European Axis and Charter of the International Military Tribunal, August 8, 1945, 82 U.N.T.S. 279) article 6. See also, Affirmation of the Principles of International Law Recognized by the Charter of the Nuremberg Tribunal, G.A. Res. 95(1). U.N. Doc. A/64/Add. 1 at 188 (1946).

158 Unocal Position Statement: "Proposed Central Asia Pipeline Projects," (1998) available on Unocal Internet site at www.unocal.com.

159 The Feminist Majority Foundation, "Stop Gender Apartheid in Afghanistan!", available on Feminist Majority Internet site at www.feminist.org.

the way to international lending agencies coming in."[160]

Gender apartheid.

At gunpoint, the Taliban have imposed the most oppressive regime of gender apartheid known to the world, banning girls from going to school, banning women from attending university, prohibiting women from holding jobs, requiring women to be accompanied at all times in public by a male member of their immediate families, requiring women to be covered from head to toe in a "burqa" with only a small mesh facial opening, forbidding women from wearing white socks or noisy shoes, and requiring windows of homes with women to be darkened.[161] Girls in an orphanage may not play outside; boys may.[162] One woman showing her ankle while riding a bicycle with her husband was shot straight through the heart by a Taliban elder.[163]

The following facts demonstrate the horrors inflicted upon women in Afghanistan:

• Women and girls are prohibited from attending schools or universities. Even private home schooling is not permitted. On June 16, The Taliban closed more than 100 privately operating home schools for girls and restricted any education to religious instruction for girls up to age eight.[164]

• After nearly two decades of war, many women in Afghanistan are war widows and the sole source of support for their families. Many of these families have been thrust into poverty as women and girls are forced to beg for food because they have no male relatives to support them and they are not allowed to support themselves. Without a male family member to accompany them at all times

---

160 "Taliban's Unlikely Story," *Moneyclips*, October 17, 1996 (Source: Al Ahram Weekly).
161 The Feminist Majority Foundation, supra note 159.
162 Id.
163 Maggie O'Kane, "A Holy Betrayal: The Taliban, Islam's Warriors, Have Launched Jihad Against Their Own Afghan Countrywomen," *The Guardian,* November 29, 1997.
164 "100 Girls' Schools in Afghan Capital Are Ordered Shut," *The New York Times,* June 17, 1998 (Associated Press).

1 many have become prisoners in their own homes.[165]

2 • Women cannot be treated by male doctors and have severely lim-
3 ited access to medical care. Barred from receiving medical treatment in hospitals, women are forced to seek care at a primitive
4 women's hospital with limited supplies, only a few beds, and no
5 running water. One woman who had suffered severe burns on 80%
of her body was denied treatment because male doctors were not
6 allowed to remove clothing from her body. Women have been shot
7 at for leaving their homes to receive medical care without a male
8 escort.[166]

9 • According to a recent study conducted by Physicians for Human
10 Rights, the women of Afghanistan have suffered serious health
consequences since the Taliban's rise to power. Of the 160 Af-
11 ghan women participating in the study, 71% reported a decline in
12 physical health and 81% a decline in mental health.[167]

13 • Many Afghan women, unable to bear the psychological and physi-
14 cal torture of their status, are committing suicide. According to
the Physicians for Human Rights study, 97% demonstrated evi-
15 dence of major depression.[168]
16

17 • Prior to the Taliban's arrival, women in Afghanistan were edu-
cated and employed: 50% of the students and 60% of the teachers
18 at Kabul University were women, and 70% of school teachers,
19 50% of civilian government workers, and 50% of doctors in Kabul
were women.[169]
20

21 _____

22 165 Nora Boustany, "Wretched Art They Amongst Women," *The Washington Post*, August 5, 1998.
23 166 Shelley Alpern, "Another Burma? Unocal Joins Forces With Brutal Afghan Regime to Further Regional Oil Pipeline," *Franklin Research's In-
24 sight*, July 1998.
167 Zohra Rasekh, MPH, et al., "Women's Health and Human Rights in Af-
25 ghanistan," *Journal of the American Medical Association*, Abstracts,
August 5, 1998.
26 168 Id.
169 Shelley Alpern, "Another Burma? Unocal Joins Forces With Brutal Af-
27 ghan Regime to Further Regional Oil Pipeline," *Franklin Research's In-
28 sight*, July 1998.

HEED 8/98

- The rights of Afghan women were fully protected by their 1963 constitution.[170]

- Under Islam, women are allowed to work, to earn and control their own money, and to participate in public life. The Taliban claim to represent fundamentalist Islamic ideology, yet their laws against women have no foundation in Islam.[171]

- For violation of the Taliban's harsh edicts women have been beaten, shot at, publicly flogged, tortured, and even killed.[172]

Overall, 98% of respondents in the Physicians for Human Rights study met the criteria for post traumatic stress disorder, major depression, or significant symptoms of anxiety, 52% met the criteria for two of these and 37% met the criteria for all three. The report concluded that the current health and human rights status of women in Afghanistan suggests that the combined effects of war-related trauma and human rights abuses by Taliban officials have had a profound negative effect on Afghan women's health.[173]

All of the above constitute an open assault on the law of Afghanistan, customary international law including *jus cogens* norms (i.e., the highest peremptory norms of international law that may never be transgressed, which proscribe both apartheid and torture), the Universal Declaration of Human Rights,[174] the International Covenant on Civil and Political Rights,[175] the International Covenant on Economic, Social and Cultural Rights,[176] the Convention on the Elimination of All Forms of Discrimination Against Women,[177] the Vienna Declaration and Program of Action,[178] and the Beijing Declaration.[179] The Taliban's

170 Id.
171 Id.
172 Id.
173 Rasekh, et al. "Women's Health and Human Rights in Afghanistan," *Journal of the American Medical Association*, August 5, 1998.
174 G.A. Res. 217A (III), U.N. Doc. A/810 (1948).
175 999 U.N.T.S. 171, 6 I.L.M. 368
176 993 U.N.T.S. 3, 6 I.L.M. 360
177 G.A.Res. 34/180, U.N.GAOR Supp. (No.46) at 193,U.N. Doc. A/34/180.
178 32 I.L.M. 1661.
179 35 I.L.M. 401.

HEED 8/98

restrictions on women have been condemned by the U.S. State Department, the European Parliament and more than 100 human rights organizations worldwide, including Islamic organizations.[180]

Unocal's liability.

Doing business with the Taliban unavoidably supports their regime of gender apartheid. As a collaborator with the Taliban, Unocal has become an integral participant in the ongoing violation of the human rights of Afghanistan's entire female population. Unocal's burgeoning Afghan business activity aids and abets the Taliban's violations specifically (a) by lending the Taliban legitimacy as a de facto government, (b) by funding training of male-only pipeline construction workers, and (c) by giving advice on oil and gas development to provide financial footing for these extremists. The Taliban stand to collect $50 million to $100 million a year in transit fees if the pipeline is built.[181] The Physicians for Human Rights study concluded that "corporate investment in Afghanistan directly and indirectly aids the Taliban regime, and contributes to the suffering of the Afghan people, especially women. For this reason PHR calls for a moratorium on investment in Afghanistan, including the oil and gas pipelines proposed by a consortium of multinational corporations, including Unocal, based in California and Bridas of Argentina."[182] Under U.S. and California law, Unocal is legally liable for these violations of the Taliban if the business dealings "lend aid or encouragement to the wrongdoer," or if Unocal uses Taliban as its "agent," or the company is a "joint participant" with Taliban in a business enterprise, or if Unocal is an "accomplice" with the Taliban in its crimes against humanity. It is also liable under common law doctrines of "negligent hiring" and "negligent supervision" for funding a pipeline worker training program that excludes females. These traditional legal doctrines are explained further below in connection with Unocal's activities in Burma.[183] Unocal is also directly liable under California law for having made a sham con-

---

180 The Feminist Majority Foundation, supra note 159.
181 Dan Morgan and David B. Ottaway, "Women's Fury Toward Taliban Stalls Pipeline," *Washington Post*, June 11, 1998 at A-1.
182 Physicians for Human Rights, *The Taliban's War on Women: A Health and Human Rights Crisis in Afghanistan* (Boston, Washington, D.C. 1998).
183 See notes 231-237 infra.

1 tract calling for non-discrimination that actually sets up a male-only
   job training program in violation of public policy, a violation of *Busi-*
2 *ness and Professions Code* § 17200.

3   Unocal has falsely denied that it is conducting business with the
   Taliban, thereby misleading its business competitors, the public, and
4 its shareholders. Its activities with the Taliban and its false and decep-
5 tive statements about those activities work a forfeiture of Unocal's
   charter because the charter has been "unlawfully exercised,"[184] and
6 "perverted,"[185] in "serious offen[se]" against "the statutes regulating
7 corporations,"[186] including the Unfair Competition Act prohibiting "any
8 unlawful, unfair or fraudulent business act or practice."[187]

9 **Unocal's version.**

10   The company declared on its web page for months or longer prior
   to July, 1998 that, "Unocal will not conduct business with any party in
11 Afghanistan until peace is achieved and a government recognized by
12 international lending agencies is in place. We have neither signed nor
   negotiated any business deals with any faction within Afghanistan."[188]
13 The statement cannot be squared with press reports. The press has
14 reported that a delegation of top Taliban officials met with Unocal in
   Texas in December 1997 to discuss the building of a pipeline. They
15 were chauffeured in a company minibus and had dinner at the home of
16 Unocal vice-president Martin Miller. Unocal paid for one of them to
17 go to an optician for eye care. They were helicoptered to an oil rig in
   the Gulf of Mexico to examine Unocal's deep-water drilling technol-
18 ogy.[189] Unocal has been sued by Bridas Corporation of Argentina in
19 Texas courts for interference with its own business deal to bring
   Turkmenistan gas through Afghanistan.[190] In February 1998 a team
20

21 ———————————
22 184 California Code of Civil Procedure § 803.
   185 *Dashaway*, supra note 69.
23 186 California Corporations Code § 1801 (a) (1).
   187 California Business & Professions Code § 17200.
24 188 Unocal Position Statement: "Proposed Central Asia Pipeline Projects,"
        available on Unocal Internet site at www.unocal.com.
25 189 Caroline Lees, "International: Oil Barons Court Taliban in Texas," *The
26   Sunday Telegraph London*, December 14, 1997; Ed Vulliamy, "U.S.
        Women Fight Taliban Oil Deal," *The Guardian Foreign Page*, January
27   12, 1998.
   190 Hugh Pope, "Pipeline Dreams: How Two Firms' Fight for Turkmenistan
28   Gas Landed in Texas Court," *The Wall Street Journal*, January 19, 1998.

from Unocal visited Kabul for four days and held talks with Taliban authorities on oil and gas exploration in Afghanistan.[191] Later, the Taliban minister of mines and industries said the CentGas consortium led by Unocal had applied to survey the 458 mile Afghan pipeline route and "the consortium want to start building the pipeline by the end of 1998."[192] A recent news report told that the Taliban and Northern Alliance factions who are fighting had agreed to cooperate on the pipeline and have "finalized two protocols between them and CentGas...."[193] An even more recent report of the Taliban's military victory over their foes quotes the Taliban deputy information minister as saying the pipeline can now go ahead and that the militia favors CentGas to do it.[194] All of these activities, of course, amount to "conducting business" and "negotiating business deals" with the Taliban.

The company's flat denial that it was conducting business with the Taliban persisted though the annual shareholders' meeting on June 1, 1998, where CEO Roger Beach continued to defend the statement against hostile shareholder questions. Suddenly, in July, 1998, without admitting its past deception, Unocal changed its story, posting a new policy on its web page statement that reads, in pertinent part:

> Unocal has not—and will not—enter into any unilateral commercial agreement with an individual Afghanistan faction, including the Taliban and Northern alliance. . . .The CentGas consortium members continue to have dialogue with all factions in Afghanistan to communicate the benefits we believe would result from building a gas pipeline through that country. . . .[I]t offers a unique potential benefit for both men and women in Afghanistan. Consistent with our core values and business principles, we are currently providing humanitarian support to Afghanistan through CARE and the University of Nebraska at Omaha. These projects. . . include basic job skills training and edu-

---

191 "US Oil Company Team Holds Talks with Taliban on Exploration Plan," *Agence France Presse*, February 14, 1998.
192 "Taliban Hope To Begin Building Afghan Pipeline by End of 1998," *Agence France Presse*, May 22, 1998.
193 "Afghan Factions Strike Deal To Build Gas Pipeline," *Itar-Tass,* June 6, 1998.
194 Mohammed Basheer, "Victorious Taliban Reopen Bid for Recognition, Pipeline," *Agence France Presse* August 11, 1998.

HEED 8/98

cation for both men and women. . . .[195]

Thus, the previous flat denial that it was "conducting business" has now degenerated to a mere assertion that it will not enter any "unilateral commercial agreement," meaning, apparently, that its multilateral CentGas consortium may nevertheless do so.

Unocal's male-only job training program.

In addition, Unocal entered a $900,000 per year contract in August 1997 with the University of Nebraska, Omaha, under which the University's Afghanistan Study Center is to provide educational programs in Afghanistan, including training of pipeline construction workers in the Taliban controlled area.[196] Unocal talks of the contract as charity on its web page: "Consistent with our core values and business principles we are currently providing humanitarian support to Afghanistan through CARE and the University of Nebraska" including "basic job skills training and education for both men and women. . . ."[197] The head of the program for the University has a more realistic appraisal. He "concedes that Unocal's primary motive for offering UNO a contract is not to promote human rights or to rebuild Afghanistan's crushed educational system, but, as he said, 'to help the company' get the pipeline built."[198] In fact, the contract calls for training in skills essential to reconstruction of the war-torn nation "and to the manpower requirements of the proposed Unocal pipeline projects."[199]

While the contract calls for adherence to United Nations guidelines forbidding gender discrimination and contemplates training of women for some programs,[200] the Taliban has in fact prohibited women from being included so the University is currently only training males

---

195 Unocal policy statement: Proposed Central Asian Gas Pipeline, July, 1998, available on Internet at www.unocal.com.
196 Kenneth Freed, *"Odd Partners in UNO's Afghan Project,"* Omaha World-Herald, October 26, 1997.
197 Unocal Internet site: www.unocal.com. This statement appears in the pre-July, 1998 and in the post-July 1998 versions.
198 Kenneth Freed, supra note 196.
199 UNO/Unocal Afghan Training & Education Project Cooperative Agreement, effective August 1, 1997, Attachment C.
200 UNO/Unocal Afghan Training & Education Project Cooperative Agreement, effective August 1, 1997.

HEED 8/98

1
2
3
4
5
6
7
8
9
10
11
12
13
14
15
16
17
18
19
20
21
22
23
24
25
26
27
28

for pipeline construction jobs.[201] Therefore, either the terms of the contract are being violated or else it is a sham contract entered and continued by the parties with full knowledge that women would not be trained in Taliban territory. Such a sham contract would be contrary to the public policy of the states of Nebraska and California and would constitute a separate violation of the California Unfair Competition Act.[202]

It appears the latter is the case. A Unocal spokeswoman recently called the University of Nebraska program "spectacular" and denied any problem with "the women's issue," [203] thus necessarily endorsing the actual sex discrimination that is taking place. The spokeswoman did announce that Unocal is discontinuing the contract after the first $900,000, but for business reasons: "She said it wouldn't be prudent for Unocal to continue funding projects relating to a pipeline that still has no immediate prospects of being built." [204] Her statement simultaneously reveals the contract's paper non-discrimination provisions to be a sham and throws stark light on the company's pious claim that it entered the deal as an act of "humanitarian support."

---

201 Telephone interviews with Mohammed Basheer, project coordinator in Nebraska, by Professor Robert Benson of Loyola Law School, Los Angeles, April 22, 1998 and June 5, 1998. The University's inability to establish any co-educational training programs under the contract has been confirmed by the U.S. State Department. Kenneth Freed & Jena Janovy, "UNO Partner Pulls Out of Afghanistan Project," *Omaha World-Herald,* June 6, 1998.
202 California Business & Professions Code § 17200.
203 Freed & Janovy, supra note 201.
204 Id. The funding willl cap at $900,000, but the initial term of the contract willl be extended to December 31, 1998. Id.

HEED 8/98

Count. 4 Complicity in Crimes Against Humanity:
Aiding Oppression of Homosexuals

On the basis of the information stated and footnoted below, petitioners believe there is strong reason for the Attorney General to find the following to be true:

The factual background of the Taliban in Afghanistan related in Count Three is incorporated here by reference as if fully set forth. The Taliban's mission not only includes denying basic freedoms to females but also putting homosexuals to death. Taliban policy is to put anyone convicted of homosexual sodomy to death by burying them alive under mud walls pushed over them by a bulldozer. Two homosexuals were recently executed in this fashion. Three others who were still alive 30 minutes after a wall was pushed over them were allowed to live, with broken bones.[205] This represented a triumph of one school of Taliban thought. Another advocated throwing homosexuals off a tall building, while a third argued merely for parading them through the streets with blackened faces.[206]

This torture and killing of homosexuals constitutes an open assault on the law of Afghanistan, customary international law including *jus cogens* norms (i.e., the highest peremptory norms of international law that may never be transgressed, which proscribe torture), the Universal Declaration of Human Rights,[207] the International Covenant on Civil and Political Rights.[208] and the International Covenant on Economic, Social and Cultural Rights.[209]

Unocal's liability. Doing business with the Taliban unavoidably supports their regime of torture and death for homosexuals, just as doing business with Nazi Germany supported the ovens of the Holocaust. As collaborator with the Taliban, Unocal has become an integral participant in the ongoing violation of the human rights of Afghanistan's entire homosexual population. Unocal's burgeoning

---

205 Sayed Salhuddin, "Asia: Taliban Execute Two People Convicted of Sodomy," *Reuters*, March 23, 1998.

206 "Taliban = Death and Humiliation for Homosexuals," *The Observer* (London), February 23, 1997.

207 G.A. Res. 217A (III), U.N. Doc. A/810 (1948).

208 999 U.N.T.S. 171, 6 I.L.M. 368.

209 993 U.N.T.S. 3, 6 I.L.M. 360.

HEED 8/98

1 Afghan business activity aids and abets the Taliban's violations specifically (a) by lending the Taliban legitimacy as a de facto govern-
2 ment, and (b) by giving advice on oil and gas development to provide
3 financial footing for these extremists. The Taliban stand to collect $50
million to $100 million a year in transit fees if the pipeline is built.[210]
4 The Physicians for Human Rights study concluded that "corporate in-
5 vestment in Afghanistan directly and indirectly aids the Taliban regime, and contributes to the suffering of the Afghan people . . . . For
6 this reason PHR calls for a moratorium on investment in Afghanistan,
7 including the oil and gas pipelines proposed by a consortium of multinational corporations, including Unocal, based in California and Bridas
8 of Argentina".[211] Under U.S. and California law, Unocal is legally li-
9 able for these violations of the Taliban if its business dealings "lend
10 aid or encouragement to the wrongdoer," or if Unocal uses Taliban as
its "agent," or the company is a "joint participant" with Taliban in a
11 business enterprise, or if Unocal is an "accomplice" with the Taliban
12 in its crimes against humanity. These traditional legal doctrines are
explained further below in connection with Unocal's activities in
13 Burma.[212]

14 As described above in Count Three, Unocal has falsely denied
that it is conducting business with the Taliban, misleading its business
15 competitors, the public, and its shareholders. Its activities with the
16 Taliban and its false and deceptive statements about those activities
17 work a forfeiture of Unocal's charter because the charter has been
"unlawfully exercised,"[213] and "perverted,"[214] in "serious offen[se]"
18 against "the statutes regulating corporations,"[215] including the Unfair
19 Competition Act prohibiting "any unlawful, unfair or fraudulent business act or practice."[216]
20

21

22

23
210 Morgan and Ottaway, supra note 181.
24 211 Physicians for Human Rights, *The Taliban's War on Women: A Health
and Human Rights Crisis in Afghanistan* (Boston, Washington, D.C.
25 1998).
26 212 See notes 231-235 infra.
213 California Code of Civil Procedure § 803.
27 214 *Dashaway*, supra note 69.
215 California Corporations Code § 1801 (a) (1).
28 216 California Business & Professions Code § 17200.

HEED 8/98

Count 5. Complicity in Crimes Against Humanity:
Enslavement and Forced Labor

On the basis of the information stated and footnoted below, petitioners believe there is strong reason for the Attorney General to find
the following to be true:

Unocal has formed a business enterprise with the illegal military
dictatorship of Burma to build a natural gas pipeline across a civil war
zone in the country. To understand how this relationship has led Unocal
to violate the law, it is necessary to recount the background of the
pipeline deal.

SLORC takes power.

Burma has spent most of the post World War II era under military
rule. However, there was renewed pro-democracy activity in Burma in
the late eighties. Burmese citizens organized politically, demanding
democracy, an end to human rights violations and, most importantly,
an end to decades of military dictatorship. The ruling military elite
brutally put down the movement, reorganized themselves and declared
a new regime on September 18, 1988, called the State Law and Order
Restoration Council (SLORC). The "new" SLORC regime imposed
martial law on Burma and renamed the country "Myanmar," a name
the democratic groups do not acknowledge.

In a bid for legitimacy in the wake of their suppression of the pro-
democracy movement, SLORC held multi-party elections on May 27,
1990. The people of Burma soundly rejected the SLORC dictatorship
in the election; the National League for Democracy (NLD), led by
Daw Aung San Suu Kyi (who was later awarded the Nobel Peace Prize),
won 82 percent of the parliamentary seats. In an act of repression which
has been universally condemned,[217] SLORC refused to relinquish its

---

217 On March 17, 1993, the UN Human Rights Commission in Geneva unani-
mously adopted a resolution condemning SLORC for "continuing extremely serious human rights violations" including torture, arbitrary ex-
ecutions, forced labor (including portering for the army), abuse of women
and politically motivated arrest and detentions. The Commission called
for an accelerated transition to democracy by convening the National
Assembly elected in 1990 and ending Daw Aung San Suu Kyi's deten-
tion. United Nations Human Rights Commission, March 17, 1993, *Burma
News,* April 1993, No. 4, Vol. 4, p. 4, available on the University of
North Carolina Internet site located at ftp://sunsite.unc.edu/pub/academic/
political-science/freeburma/ba/.

military rule after the election. Since 1990 NLD leaders have been arrested, killed or exiled and repression of the pro-democracy movement has only intensified.

Yadana oil field deal begins.

The entities building the Yadana pipeline in Burma have been, by their own admission, purposely organized as a corporation.[218] The corporation's component companies began planning for the pipeline prior to any individual company's signing a deal with a representative of the SLORC regime. Member companies Unocal and Total began negotiating with SLORC for oil and gas exploration deals in Burma not later than 1991. Total, a French company and lead partner in the corporation, was awarded its bid for the Yadana concession in 1992.[219] Unocal officially joined the project in 1993 when the corporate entity, the Moattama Gas Transportation Company (MGTC) was formed. MGTC is composed of Total, with a 31.24% share; Unocal, through a wholly owned subsidiary, with a 28.26% share; PTT Exploration and Production Public Co., Ltd of Thailand, with a 25.5% share; and the Myanmar Oil & Gas Enterprise (MOGE), a wholly owned subsidiary of SLORC, with a 15% share.

In late 1989 Unocal began pouring millions of dollars into the SLORC regime. In 1989, less than a year after the pro-democracy movement was crushed and just months before the elections which SLORC has to this day not honored, Unocal paid SLORC $5-8 million to secure rights on large exploration blocks for oil and gas. During the 1990-1992 period Unocal was not a disinterested observer of the Yadana oil field development, but rather was concurrently conducting an unsuccessful onshore exploration program in central Burma.[220]

---

218 Statement of Unocal Corporation for the Department of Labor Report to Congress—Labor Conditions in Burma at the Yadana Pipeline February 1998, p. 1, available on the Unocal Internet site (February 1998) www.unocal.com/Myanmar/labor.htm.

219 Constructive Engagement In Myanmar, Testimony submitted to the U.S. Senate Banking Committee on S. 1511, May 22, 1996, by John Imle, President of Unocal Corporation, available on the Unocal Internet site (February 1998) www.unocal.com.

220 Earth Rights International (ERI) and Southeast Asia Information Network (SAIN), *Total Denial: A Report on the Yadana Pipeline Project in Burma* (1996) Appendix A "Chronology of Burma's Natural Gas Development," at 66.

SLORC began preparing the land for the pipeline in 1991, while negotiating with Unocal and Total. SLORC began building permanent military outposts in the area of the proposed pipeline. In fact, the confiscation of land, relocation of villages and destruction of rainforest and other habitat in the pipeline region began when business negotiations began,[221] although the 30-year gas sales contract and pipeline agreement calling for deliveries of natural gas to Thailand beginning in mid-1998 was not signed until February 1995.[222]

Violations of law.

As part of the pipeline enterprise, Unocal has profited from the use of forced and slave labor, in violation of customary international law, the Universal Declaration of Human Rights,[223] the International Covenant on Civil and Political Rights, [224] the International Covenant on Economic, Social and Cultural Rights,[225] the International Labor Organization Convention No. 29 Concerning Forced or Compulsory Labor,[226] the International Labor Organization Convention No. 105 Concerning the Abolition of Forced Labor,[227] the Slavery Convention,[228] the Protocol Amending the Slavery Convention,[229] and the Conven-

---

221 Unocal, has argued that its involvement in the Yadana pipeline project began in 1993 and that as of 1996 its relocation and compensation program was not fully underway. In 1996, Unocal issued a "statement to correct false allegations concerning the Yadana Project in Myanmar," stating: "All land required for the pipeline project will be purchased from local landowners, based on potential maximum crop yields, actual crop loss, and other factors. Under this policy, more than 300 villagers will be paid $1 million to acquire the 525 acres of land required for project infrastructure, roads, pipeline center and right-of-way. No land will be taken without fair compensation to the owners." Unfortunately for Burmese villagers, by late 1996 most of the relocation, habitat destruction and theft had already taken place. December 12, 1996, News Release, available on Unocal Internet site www.unocal.com/uclnews/96htm/.
222 "Unocal announces new Myanmar gas discovery," March 5, 1996, News Release, available on Unocal Internet site www.unocal.com/uclnews/96htm/.
223 G.A. Res. 217A (III), U.N. Doc. A/810 (1948).
224 999 U.N.T.S. 171, 6 I.L.M. 368.
225 993 U.N.T.S. 3, 6 I.L.M. 360.
226 39 U.N.T.S. 55 .
227 320 U.N.T.S. 291.
228 46 Stat. 2183, T.S. No. 788. 60 I.N.T.S. 253.
229 7. U.S. T. 479.

tion on the Rights of the Child.[230]

Unocal is liable for these violations by its military business partner under traditional doctrines of, conspiracy,[231] agency,[232] joint par-

---

230 28 I.L.M. 1448.

231 "All those who, in pursuance of a common plan or design to commit a tortious act, actively take part in it, or further it by cooperation or request, or who lend aid or encouragement to the wrongdoer, or ratify and adopt his acts done for their benefit, are equally liable with him. Express agreement is not necessary, and all that is required is that there be a tacit understanding. . . . It is connection with such vicarious liability that the word conspiracy is often used. . . .[T]he word gradually came to be used to extend liability in tort, as well as crime, beyond the active wrongdoer to those who have merely planned, assisted or encouraged his acts." William L. Prosser, *Law of Torts* § 46 (4th ed., 1971).

232 "A private corporation is ordinarily liable under the doctrine of *respondeat superior* for torts of its agents or employees committed while they are acting within the scope of their employment." 5 Witkin, *Summary of California Law: Torts* § 37 (9th ed., 1988). "Liability under the doctrine of *respondeat superior* extends to malicious acts and other intentional torts . . . ." 2 Witkin, *Summary of California Law: Agency and Employment* § 135. "An employer is liable for an assault and battery committed by an employee where the employment in some way involves the risks of force used against third persons. . . . The same is true when an employee in charge of property defends it by the use of excessive force." Id. at § 136.

233 The Alien Tort Claims Act (ATCA), 28 U.S.C. § 1350, gives the federal courts jurisdiction over torts committed against aliens in violation of international law. Even if international law is understood narrowly to cover only acts by nations, private actors are liable when they are joint participants with governments that commit the violations. "Thus, where there is a 'substantial degree of cooperative action' between the state and private actors in effecting the deprivation of rights" [liability attaches to both]. . . . Here, plaintiffs allege that SLORC and MOGE are agents of the private defendants; that the defendants are joint venturers, working in concert with one another; and that the defendants have conspired to commit the violations of international law alleged in the complaint in order to further the interests of the Yadana gas pipeline project. Additional factual inquiry is not necessary. Plaintiffs have alleged that the private plaintiffs were and are jointly engaged with the state officials in the challenged activity, namely forced labor and other human rights violations in furtherance of the pipeline project. These allegations are sufficient to support subject-matter jurisdiction under the ATCA." *John Doe I et al. v. Unocal et al.,* Order Granting in Part and Denying in Part Defendant Unocal's Motion to Dismiss, March 27, 1997 (U.S. Dist. Court, Central Dist. Cal., Case No. CV 96-6959 RAP (BQRx) at 21-22).

ticipation[233] and crimes against humanity.[234] Unocal is also directly liable for these acts under the common-law torts of negligence,[235] negligent hiring[236] and negligent supervision.[237] As the previous seven footnotes confirm, there is nothing radical or legally unusual about holding Unocal liable for its business partner's violations. The legal doctrines are ancient and commonplace, applied in U.S. courts every day. Now that corporations are more often acting globally, it is to be expected that the site of their harms will be distant places. But the foreign locale does not change the traditional law applicable to determine their liability.

Unocal knew or should have known and could have reasonably foreseen that its military partner would use forced labor to clear the land for the pipeline route, build related infrastructure in the area, and provide security for the pipeline.

• The latest U.S. State Department report observes:

> Forced or compulsory labor remains a serious problem. In March following an investigation of the country's forced labor practices, the European Union Commission revoked benefits under the Generalized System of Preferences. In recent years, the SLORC has increasingly supplemented declining gross investment with uncompensated people's "contributions," chiefly of forced labor, to build or maintain irrigation, transportation and tourism infrastructure projects. During 1996 the Government introduced an initiative to use military personnel for infrastructure projects. This initiative and the increasing use of heavy construction equip-

---

234 Individual private citizens who were "organizers" or "accomplices" were among those indictable for crimes against humanity under the tribunals that sat at Nuremberg and Tokyo after World War II. The war crimes tribunals currently set up to try defendants in the former Yugoslavia and in Rwanda have similar jurisdiction.

235 "An act or omission may be negligent if the actor realizes or should realize that it involves an unreasonable risk of harm to another through the conduct of the other or a third person which is intended to cause harm, even though such conduct is criminal." American Law Institute, *Restatement of the Law (Second) : Torts* § 302B. "Factors to be considered are the known character, past conduct, and tendencies of the person whose intentional conduct causes the harm. . . ." Id. , Comment f.

236 Id. § 411.

237 Id. § 415.

HEED 8/98

ment resulted in a decline during 1996-97 in the use of unpaid labor on physical infrastructure projects, especially for irrigation projects and railroad building. Nonetheless, there were credible reports that the use of forced labor remained widespread throughout the country. The army continued to force citizens—including women and children—to work as porters. . . . The Government does not specifically prohibit forced and bonded labor by children. . . . In March the governing board of the ILO established a Commission of Inquiry to investigate Burma for its violation of ILO Convention 29 on forced labor. The complaint accuses the Government of systematic use of forced labor.[238]

- The mistreatment of porters has been well documented by observers, and constitutes torture and cruel, inhuman and degrading treatment in addition to the extraction of forced labor.[239] SLORC military rulers have sought to justify the use of slave labor by refer-

---

238 U.S. Department of State, *Burma Country Report on Human Rights Practices for 1997* at § 6 c. (Jan. 30, 1998). See also U.N. Economic and Social Council, Commission on Human Rights, *1998 Situation of Human Rights in Myanmar* (April 20, 1998); Amnesty International, *Myanmar Portering & Forced Labour: Amnesty International's Concerns* (Sept. 1996).

239 Human Rights Watch/Asia, *Human Rights Developments and the Need for Continued Pressure,* at 8-9, available from Human Rights Watch's Internet site www.hrw.org. See also, U.S. Department of State, *Burma Report on Human Rights Practices for 1996,* January 30, 1997, and *The Nation,* Bangkok, June 23, 1993 [quoted in Burma News, July 1993, No. 7, Volume 4, available at the University of North Carolina Internet site ftp://sunsite.unc.edu/pub/academic/political-science/freeburma/ba/. / Burma/ab2800.htm.]: "The ill-treatment of both men and women porters has been documented. Yet SLORC continues to deny the practice. On 9 Apr, SLORC stated that all labour provided by villagers for the Army is voluntary and that 'porters recruited are never required to accompany the troops to the actual scene of battles; neither are they exposed to danger.' However, since the beginning of the year, decapitated bodies of porters bayoneted or beaten have been seen floating down the Salween river from SLORC-controlled areas. A villager who lives ten kilometers downstream from Saw Hta estimates that 200 bodies have floated past his house in the last 5 months. 'They were all porters. I would say many of them were Shan villagers because they were wearing the traditional Shan pants. About a quarter of them were women. They are usually without clothes. I think the women are raped before being killed.' "

ence to Burmese custom and cultural practice[240] and have attempted to convince the international community that its use of forced labor is in compliance with international law. Since MGTC began the Yadana pipeline project the use of forced labor in Burma has increased:

> As the SLORC has opened up the economy to international investors, it has forced civilians and prisoners to rebuild the country's infrastructure, which was badly neglected by the previous government. The SLORC claims that these "development projects" are designed for the long-term benefit of all, because they will create the infrastructure for improvements in the standards of living of their people. Human Rights Watch/Asia estimates that since 1992 *at least two million people* have been forced to work without pay on the construction of roads, railways and bridges across the country. Hundreds have died from beatings, exhaustion, accidents and lack of medical care. The use of unpaid civilians on these development projects is a violation of the 1930 International Labor Organization (ILO) Convention, to which Burma is a signatory. In violation of Common Article 3 of the Geneva Conventions, forced labor has also been used for overtly military practices. This includes the use of civilians as porters for the army, to construct army barracks, and to stand watch on roads and railways in areas where ethnic rebels are active. [Emphasis added][241]

•In November 1994 the International Labor Organization investigated the use of forced labor in Burma and found: "[T]he extraction of labor and services, in particular porterage service, under the village Act and the Towns Act is contrary to the Forced Labor Convention, 1930 (No. 29), ratified by the government of Myanmar in 1955."[242] In June 1995, the ILO's committee of Experts on the Application of Conventions and Recommendations rejected the

---

240 The military regime prefers to characterize the labor as "donated," and voluntarily contributed to the state as a "noble act of charity." According to SLORC, Burmese citizens are "voluntarily cooperating in the various development projects across the country. These citizens did not even ask for money because they would consider it an insult." Human Rights Watch/Asia, supra note 239 at 8.
241 Id. at 8.
242 Id. at 9.

HEED 8/98

SLORC's attempt to justify its use of forced labor under the criteria of the convention. International condemnation continued in December 1996 when the European Commission recommended that the European Union suspend the preferential trade tariffs which Burma then received as a developing country "until such time as forced labour practices are abolished."[243]

• According to figures published in SLORC's own paper, the *New Light of Myanmar*, as of December 15, 1993, approximately 921,753 people had worked on the Pakokku-Monywa railway without pay. In another instance SLORC stated that 799,447 people worked without pay on the Aungban-Loikaw railway.[244]

In its defense Unocal has touted the economic benefit the Yadana pipeline is bringing to the people of Burma. Yet by the company's own admission the number of direct paid employees Unocal has hired on the project numbers only between 300 and 600 Burmese, the number varying depending on the season.[245] According to human rights observers these *paid* workers were not recruited until March 1995, long after pipeline related activities began. Even then, among those living in the pipeline region, only members of the Union Solidarity and Development Association ("USDA"), SLORC's political association, were eligible for paid employment.[246]

The balance of labor on the pipeline was extracted by SLORC with force from the people of Burma. Prior to March 1995, before any pipes were laid, forced labor was used to clear a path for the pipeline and to construct infrastructure to support SLORC's natural gas development program. To facilitate building the pipeline from the Andaman Sea across the ethnic states of southern Burma, the Ye-Tavoy railway line was begun to transport troops and supplies to the pipeline area. In October 1993, it was reported that up to 2,000 people a day were being forced to labor on the railway.[247]

---

243 Human Rights Watch/Asia, *Burma, Children's Rights and the Rule of Law*, (January 1997), available from Human Rights Watch's Internet site located at http://www.hrw.org..

244 *Total Denial* supra note 220 at 8.

245 *Asia Times*, "Why Unocal Ignores Myanmar Sanctions," August 13, 1996, at 9.

246 *Total Denial*, supra note 74, at 8.

247 Id. at 13. Ye-Tavoy railway crosses Ye Byu, which is one of the townships through which the pipeline will pass.

The Ye-Tavoy railway is a nexus of cruel, inhuman and degrading treatment, all precipitated by the Yadana pipeline project.

• Human Rights Watch/Asia published the following report on abuses suffered by those working on the Ye-Tavoy railway that are being carried out for Unocal's economic profit:

A twenty-eight-year-old man interviewed by Human Rights Watch/Asia in a refugee camp in Thailand in May 1994 described conditions for forced laborers at the Ye-Tavoy railway, one of the most notorious construction site[s] in Burma, and one on which work continued in January 1996:

"It was very difficult for families like mine which have only one man. When I was at the work site, the rest of my family found it difficult to work the farm and grow food. When a man returns, women are expected to replace him at the work site ... I saw some elderly people working there and some children aged about twelve years. I also saw some pregnant women working there. . . One girl from Moe Gyi village who was four and half months pregnant died from malnutrition and diarrhea in mid-March 1994. She did not get any medical help. People were beaten by soldiers for trying to escape or for not working hard enough. Some people attempted to flee from the work site but were caught. They were beaten and tortured in front of everyone."

In September 1995, a report in a British newspaper confirmed that twelve-year-old children were still working on this same railway project. The article included an interview with a Karen man who had worked on the railway who said "labourers encouraged children at the site to rest, but the soldiers beat them and ordered them to work. Some children were as young as twelve." In January 1995 a woman from Karen state interviewed by Human Rights Watch/Asia said, "Sometimes we didn't go because we were tired, and they [the soldiers] came and dragged us from the our house. My children were screaming and crying, but I just had to leave them there." This is a common problem, it seems, as increasing numbers of people are taken to work for the military. In many cases, women with babies who are still suckling have to take their babies with them, tied to their backs as they do heavy work such as breaking rocks or digging trenches.[248]

• EarthRights International and Southeast Asian Information Network have also documented with testimony of Burmese victims that forced labor has been used on projects directly for the pipeline and on related infrastructure projects.[249] This is in addition to the forced portering for the military providing security in the pipeline area.

• Two lawsuits against Unocal filed in federal court in Los Angeles contain similar allegations.[250]

Unocal's response and damning admission.

Unocal likes to quote the U.S. State Department report on Burma for 1996 which addressed the pipeline with this remark: "The preponderance of the evidence indicates that the pipeline project has paid its workers at least a market wage." [251] The comment leaves open the possibility that, though paid, the labor was nevertheless forced, and it says nothing about related infrastructure projects or military security.

The company has made a number of contradictory and finely shaved statements on the issue. It has said: "From initial clearing, grading and infrastructure development, through constructing, laying and burying the onshore pipeline, all work has been done by voluntary labor under formal contracts. Workers receive their pay directly, with receipt stringently documented. Unocal has sent representatives to the project; their observations confirm Total's reports: there has never been forced labor on the pipeline; we would never countenance it."[252] The same statement, however, makes clear that Unocal does not consider work on the Ye-Tavoy railroad or other local infrastructure projects to

---

248 *Burma, Children's Rights and the Rule of Law*, supra note 243.
249 *Total Denial* supra note 220.
250 *John Doe I et al. v. Unocal Corp. et al.,* Case No. 96-6959 (U.S. Dist. Court Central Dist. Cal., filed Oct. 1996), *National Coalition Government of Burma et al. v. Unocal,* Case No. 96-6112RAP (U.S. Dist. Court Central Dist. Cal., filed Sept. 1996. Both cases have been allowed to proceed to discovery. *John Doe I et al. v. Unocal et al.,* Order of March 27, 1997; *National Coalition,* order of November 5, 1997.
251 U.S. Department of State, *Burma Country Report on Human Rights Practices for 1996* at 12 (Jan. 30, 1997).
252 Statement of Unocal Corporation for the Department of Labor Report to Congress, February 1998, available on Unocal web site www.unocal.com.

be related to the pipeline and does not consider military security for the pipeline relevant. But Unocal President John Imle also told a group of human rights activists in 1995: "Let's be reasonable about this, what I'm saying is that if you threaten the pipeline, there's going to be more military. If forced labor goes hand-in-glove with the military, yes, there will be more forced labor."[253] Imle later backtracked in an interview with *Infrastructure Finance* magazine: "The troops assigned to provide security on our pipeline are not using forced labor."[254] Then, in a sworn deposition in the *John Doe I* lawsuit,[255] Imle confirmed that Total told him Total paid for military porters. That necessarily means they were paid for pipeline purposes. And even when workers are paid, they are not necessarily voluntary workers. Imle then made this damning admission:

> Surrounding the question of porters for the military and their payment was the issue of whether they were conscripted or volunteer workers. The consensus--although very had to verify this--but the consensus was that it was mixed. Some porters were conscripted.[256]

On this evidence, the Attorney General has abundant "reason to believe" that Unocal is benefiting from and liable for the use of forced labor to construct, support, or protect the pipeline, or all of these. These violations work a forfeiture of Unocal's corporate charter because the charter has been "unlawfully exercised,"[257] and "perverted,"[258] in "serious offen[se]" against "the statutes regulating corporations,"[259] including the Unfair Competition Act prohibiting "any unlawful, unfair or fraudulent business act or practice."[260]

253 *Total Denial*, supra note 220 at 32, citing transcript of a meeting of January 4, 1995.
254 Id., citing Gregory Millman, "Troubling Projects," *Infrastructure Finance*, Feb/March 1996 at 18.
255 Supra note 250.
256 Deposition of John Imle, President of Unocal Corp., August 14-15, 1997, in *John Doe I et al. v. Unocal et al.*, supra note 250.
257 California Code of Civil Procedure § 803.
258 *Dashaway*, supra note 69.
259 California Corporations Code § 1801 (a) (1).
260 California Business & Professions Code § 17200.

HEED 8/98

Count 6. Complicity in Crimes Against Humanity: Forced Relocation of Burmese Villages and Villagers

On the basis of the information stated and footnoted below, petitioners believe there is strong reason for the Attorney General to find the following to be true:

The relevant paragraphs from Count Five, supra, describing Unocal's business enterprise to build a pipeline in Burma are incorporated here by reference as if fully set forth.

As part of the pipeline enterprise, Unocal has knowingly profited from the large-scale forcible relocation of Burmese villages and villagers without compensation, in violation of the law of Burma, customary international law, the Universal Declaration of Human Rights,[261] the International Covenant on Civil and Political Rights, [262] and the International Covenant on Economic, Social and Cultural Rights.[263]

Unocal is liable for these violations by its military business partner under traditional doctrines of conspiracy, agency, joint participation and crimes against humanity. Unocal is also directly liable for these acts under the common-law torts of negligence, negligent hiring and negligent supervision.[264]

Unocal knew or should have known and could have reasonably foreseen that its military partner would steal property and food from villagers and would forcibly relocate whole villages without compensation, creating a flood of refugees to Thailand.

• The U.S. State Department report:

> The military authorities also continued the widespread and frequent practice of forcible relocation of rural villages in ethnic minority areas in response to security concerns. This practice was particularly widespread and egregious in the Shan, Kayah, and Karen states, where tens of thousands of villagers were displaced or herded into smaller settlements in strategic areas. . . . In rural areas, military personnel at times confiscated livestock and food supplies.[265]

---

261 G.A. Res. 217A (III), U.N. Doc. A/810 (1948).
262 999 U.N.T.S. 171, 6 I.L.M. 368.
263 993 U.N.T.S. 3, 6 I.L.M. 360.
264 *See* notes 231-237 supra.
265 U.S. Department of State, *Burma Country Report on Human Rights Practices for 1997* at § 1 f. (January 30, 1998).

• The U.N. Commission on Human Rights has also condemned the "arbitrary seizures of land and property" and the "systematic programs of forced relocation."[266]

• EarthRights International and Southeast Asian Information Network have gathered evidence of forced village relocations.[267]

• The *John Doe I* lawsuit filed in Los Angeles alleges similar facts.[268]

Around 1991 the forced relocation of Burmese villages and villagers to secure the region for the pipeline project began. Unocal acknowledges that relocations took place but argues the villages "were nowhere near the pipeline" and took place "well before Unocal, through its affiliated subsidiary, acquired any interest in the Yadana project."[269] The three villages Unocal acknowledges, Mi Chaung Long, Lauk Thein and Yaboo, were apparently relocated in 1992 while Unocal was doing business in Burma just a year before it formally entered the Yadana project; all three villages are near the route of the Ye-Tavoy Railway which crosses the pipeline.[270] A "Humanitarian Report" prepared at Unocal's request by two outside observers acknowledges that the village of Migyaunglaung was relocated in 1991, when the SLORC took the mostly Karen people from the East Bank of the village for "security reasons" and moved them to the West Bank. After this relocation had been accomplished, Total came to the village.[271]

By late 1994 SLORC had embarked on a code-named military operation to relocate villages in the pipeline region:

> Operation Natmin [Spirit King] had two main objectives: securing the pipeline route and removing resistance forces. By the time Operation Natmin ended in July 1995, thousands of civilians had been forcibly relocated and military

---

266 U.N. Economic and Social Council, Commission on Human Rights, *1998 Situation of Human Rights in Myanmar* (April 20, 1998).
267 *Total Denial*, supra note 220 at 41-43.
268 Supra note 250.
269 Statement of Unocal Corporation, supra note 252.
270 Id.
271 Commission for Justice and Peace, *Humanitarian Report: Yadana Project* (1998), available on Unocal Internet site at www.unocal.com/myanmar/timm.htm

offensives had been conducted against several ethnic armed groups. Not surprisingly, thousands of people had also fled from the Tenasserim area to the Thai/Burmese border seeking sanctuary.[272]

If any doubt remained about the relocation of villages to accommodate the pipeline, it was removed by a half-page advertisement in the *Bankok Post* on April 17, 1995, paid for by the Electricity Generating Authority of Thailand, the major purchaser of Yadana pipeline gas. The ad trumpeted:

> The Myanmar government aims to complete its part of the gas pipeline system by 1996. . . . Myanmar has recently cleared the way by relocating a total of 11 Karen villages that would otherwise obstruct the passage of the gas resource development project.[273]

These violations work a forfeiture of Unocal's corporate charter because the charter has been "unlawfully exercised,"[274] and "perverted,"[275] in "serious offen[se]" against "the statutes regulating corporations,"[276] including the Unfair Competition Act prohibiting "any unlawful, unfair or fraudulent business act or practice."[277]

272 *Total Denial*, supra note 220 at 15, citing *Bangkok Post*, February 25, 1995.
273 Id. at 42.
274 California Code of Civil Procedure § 803.
275 *Dashaway*, supra note 69.
276 California Corporations Code § 1801 (a) (1).
277 California Business & Professions Code § 17200.

HEED 8/98

Count 7. Complicity in Crimes Against Humanity:
Killings, Torture and Rape

On the basis of the information stated and footnoted below, petitioners believe there is strong reason for the Attorney General to find the following to be true:

The relevant paragraphs from Count Five, supra, describing Unocal's business enterprise to build a pipeline in Burma are incorporated here by reference as if fully set forth. In furthering the project and protecting the pipeline, Unocal's military business partner has committed widespread killings, torture and rapes in violation of the law of Burma, customary international law, the Geneva Convention Relative to the Protection of Civilian Persons in Time of War,[278] the United Nations Charter,[279] the Universal Declaration of Human Rights,[280] the International Covenant on Civil and Political Rights,[281] the Declaration on the Protection of All Persons From Being Subjected to Torture and Other Cruel, Inhuman or Degrading Treatment or Punishment,[282] and the Convention on the Elimination of All Forms of Discrimination Against Women.[283]

Unocal is liable for these violations by its military and business partner under traditional common-law doctrines of conspiracy and agency, and under international law doctrines of joint participation and individual responsibility for crimes against humanity. Unocal is also directly liable for these acts under the common-law torts of negligence, negligent hiring, and negligent supervision.[284]

These violations work a forfeiture of Unocal's corporate charter because the charter has been "unlawfully exercised,"[285] and "perverted,"[286] in "serious offen[se]" against "the statutes regulating cor-

---

278 T.I.A.S. No. 3365.
279 59 Stat. 1031, 3 Bevans 1153 (1945).
280 G.A. Res. 217(III), U.N. Doc. A/810 (1948).
281 999 U.N.T.S. 171,6 I.L.M. 368
282 G.A. Res. 3452, 30 U.N. Doc., GAOR Supp. (No. 34) at 91, U.N. Doc. A/10034 (1976).
283 G.A. Res. 34/180, U.N.GAOR Supp. (No.46) at 193, U.N. Doc. A/34/180.
284 See notes 231-237 supra.
285 California Code of Civil Procedure § 803.
286 Dashaway, supra note 69.

HEED 8/98

porations,"[287] including the Unfair Competition Act which prohibits "any unlawful, unfair or fraudulent business act or practice."[288]

Legal liability for such violations turns on what Unocal "knew or should have known" and could have "reasonably foreseen" about its business partner's behavior. At the time Unocal was negotiating for the pipeline deal, after it was signed, and continuing today, Unocal has to have known that it was dealing with a notorious outlaw regime condemned worldwide for heinous human rights violations.

• The U. S. State Department reports during the period were unequivocal. The latest report is typical:

> Burma continued to be ruled by a highly authoritarian military regime. . . . The Government's longstanding severe repression of human rights continued during the year. . . There continue to be credible reports, particularly in ethnic minority-dominated areas, that soldiers committed serious human rights abuses, including extrajudicial killings and rape.[289]

• The U.N. Commission on Human Rights issued similar reports, of which the latest is likewise typical:

> The Commission on Human Rights . . . expresses its deep concern (a) At the continuing violations of human rights in Myanmar as reported by the Special Rapporteur, including extrajudicial, summary or arbitrary executions and enforced disappearances, torture, abuse of women and children by government agents. . . (c) At the violations of the rights of women. . . in particular forced labor, sexual violence and exploitation, including rape, as reported by the Special Rapporteur.[290]

• Amnesty International has reported on the killing, torture and rapes of civilians forced to become military porters and laborers.[291]

---

287 California Corporations Code § 1801 (a) (1).
288 California Business & Professions Code § 17200.
289 U.S. Department of State, *Burma Country Report on Human Rights Practices for 1997* at 1-2 (January 30, 1998).
290 U.N. Economic and Social Council, Commission on Human Rights, *1998 Situation of Human Rights in Myanmar* (April 20, 1998).
291 Amnesty International, *Myanmar Portering & Forced Labour: Amnesty International's Concerns* (September 1996).

HEED 8/98

• EarthRights International and Southeast Asian Information Network collaborated to gather first-person accounts of the human rights abuses connected to the pipeline's construction and protection, including killings, torture and rape, by interviewing victims inside Burma and in Thailand refugee areas.[292]

• The two lawsuits in federal court in Los Angeles allege that Unocal knew or should have known about the violations of its partner, including killings, torture and rape, and is legally responsible for them.[293]

Protecting the pipeline.

Unocal's unfair business practices are the threshold to their participation in the Yadana project. All parties in MGTC entered their business collaboration aware of the critical need to secure the pipeline and the land in which it lay in order to secure their present and future profits. To provide security, Unocal, SLORC, Total and PTTEP devised a plan to suppress anti-SLORC ethnic residents in the pipeline region. SLORC also extended a World War II-era railway, building a line from Ye in the Mon State to Tavoy in the Tenasserim region to facilitate SLORC troop movement and transport machinery and equipment needed for security.[294]

Civil war zone.

Unocal is complicit in SLORC's business strategy because it is

---

292 Supra note 220.
293 *John Doe I et al. v. Unocal Corp. et al.*, Case No. 96-6959 (U.S. Dist. Court Central Dist. Cal., filed Oct. 1996), *National Coalition Government of Burma et al. v. Unocal*, Case No. 96-6112RAP (U.S. Dist. Court Central Dist. Cal., filed Sept. 1996 [rape not pleaded in this complaint]).
294 *Bangkok Post Weekly Review*, May 13, 1994, available in Burma News, May 1994, No. 5, Vol. 5, p. 3, available on the University of North Carolina Internet site ftp://sunsite.unc.edu/pub/academic/political-science/freeburma/ba/.

HEED 8/98

part of MGTC's business plan for the pipeline. The area through which the Yadana pipeline passes has been in a state of violent civil unrest throughout Unocal's involvement in Burma.[295] MGTC planned to do business in a war zone. New military camps were added to existing military outposts along the railway route after the deal was secured.[296] The Ye-Tavoy railway, which runs perpendicular to the pipeline, is a crucial North-South transport and business expenditure for MGTC because it allows SLORC troops access to control the ethnic homelands along the East-West lying pipeline.

The military component of Unocal's business deal is undeniable. SLORC has provided an exceptionally strong and visible military presence along the route since clearing the forest before construction began:

> A full-strength battalion has approximately 800 troops. While SLORC battalions typically number only 400 soldiers, the battalions in the pipeline region are reportedly closer to full strength. Thus, with LIBs [Light Infantry Battalions] #273, #408, #409 and #410 permanently based on the pipeline route itself, *there are at least 3,000 SLORC troops designated exclusively to protect the pipeline route.* As they are reinforced by at least ten other battalions patrolling the area it is likely that the total number of troops charged with pipeline security is **over 10,000.** Such figures do not include SLORC intelligence units, police units or special forces which are also scattered throughout the region. [Emphasis added.][297]

The purpose of these troops has never been in question; their presence has allowed SLORC troops to take control of previously ethnic-controlled territory. According to the human rights reports cited above, residents of the pipeline region are indiscriminately attacked by SLORC, whether they are combatants or civilians.[298] After a February 1996 attack on Total's headquarters in Oh Bin Gain, the SLORC army

---

295 *Total Denial,* supra note 220 at 13.
296 Id.
297 Id.
298 The Geneva Convention Relative to the Protection of Civilian Persons in Time of War, done August 12, 1949, T.I.A.S., No. 3365, was deposited by Burma on August 25, 1992.

summarily executed at least ten Karen villagers from En Da Y Z Village, which is on the pipeline route.[299]

Unocal's consent to violence.

Most damning to Unocal, however, is that it and its corporate partners *expect* SLORC to use military force to protect MGTC's investment. Unocal knew or should have known that SLORC security for the pipeline would lead to human rights violations and death. According to John Imle, President of Unocal:

> There are military units there to provide security for the pipeline, surveying and eventually construction crews. There was an attack in March 1995 and one earlier this year. Of course, those attacks require security forces to be in that area. We do not pay the army for that security. It just goes with being there.[300]

Unocal's consent to the use of violence to protect the pipeline demonstrates its willingness to sacrifice human rights for profits. Unocal, pursuing lucre, came to the civil unrest in Burma; its economic investment has only exacerbated it. Total executives have also admitted to a security arrangement for MGTC with SLORC, conceding: "we know there might be a problem . . . [o]bviously the government has told us that they will make the area safe," and "unless the area is pacified, the pipeline won't last for its thirty year duration." John Imle has even said, "If you threaten the pipeline there's gonna be more military . . . *for every threat to the pipeline there will be reaction.*" [Emphasis added][301]

Liability.

It is one thing to receive police protection from a legitimate government for your business investment. It is quite another to go into

---

299 *Total Denial,* supra note 220 at 15.   None of these people were ever charged with a crime or offense.   Likewise, none received a trial, a hearing or even an informal opportunity to defend him or herself before being executed.

300 Interview with John F. Imle, President of Unocal, *Asia Times,* August 13, 1996.

301 Transcript, "Meeting on January 4, 1995 with Unocal's President and a Group Interested in the Pipeline," cited in *Total Denial,* supra note 220 at 20.

1   business with a criminal government knowing full well that it will
    protect the business through criminal means. Yet Unocal does not see
2   the difference and disavows responsibility for SLORC'S actions:

3   Unocal is not responsible for alleged acts of soldiers forc-
4   ing citizens to provide labor on unrelated government
            projects. Those who make such charges do not and cannot
5   explain how Unocal or MGTC could prevent the Burmese
            military from employing forced labor in its own ranks. There
6   is no theory under which MGTC (much less Unocal or any
7   MGTC shareholder) is responsible for such actions. In no
            way can a business (or a shareholder) be held liable for acts
8   of a government or governmental authority, even in the area
9   where the business operates. It is not done in this country;
            it would be absurd to attempt to do so elsewhere.[302]
10

11 Mr. Imle is mistaken. There are such theories and they are routinely
    applied to business partners and others in this country: conspiracy,
12 agency, joint participation, individual responsibility for crimes against
13 humanity, and negligence.[303]

14

15

16

17

18 ——————————

19

20

21

22

23

24 302 Statement of Unocal Corporation, supra note 252. In contrast, Levi-Strauss
        & Co., which pulled out of Burma in 1992, has stated publicly that "it is
25   not possible to do business in Burma without directly supporting the mili-
        tary government and its pervasive violations of human rights." "Califor-
26   nia, Connecticut and Vermont consider Burma Ban," available on the
27   University of North Carolina Internet site ftp://sunsite.unc.edu/pub/aca-
        demic/ political-science/freeburma/ba/. /Burma/ab2800.htm.
28 303 See notes 231-237 supra.

Count 8. Complicity in Gradual Cultural Genocide
of Tribal and Indigenous Peoples

On the basis of the information stated and footnoted below, petitioners believe there is strong reason for the Attorney General to find the following to be true:

The Lubicon Cree People of Canada.

In its disregard for the rights of the indigenous Lubicon Cree people, Unocal has violated recognized principles of international law expressed in the Universal Declaration of Human Rights,[304] the International Covenant on Civil and Political Rights,[305] the International Covenant on Economic, Social and Cultural Rights,[306] the International Labor Organization Convention No. 169 Concerning Indigenous and Tribal Peoples in Independent Countries,[307] the U.N. Draft Declaration on the Rights of Indigenous Peoples,[308] and the Proposed American Declaration on the Rights of Indigenous Peoples.[309] Among those principles Unocal has violated in the course of its routine business practices are:

• The right "not to be subjected to ethnocide and cultural genocide."[310]

• A prohibition against "any action which has the aim or effect of dispossessing them [indigenous peoples] of their lands, territories or resources."[311]

• The right of indigenous peoples "to own, develop, control and use the lands and territories, including the total environment of the

---

304 G.A. Res. 217(iii), U.N. Doc. A/810 (1948).
305 999 U.N.T.S. 171, 6 I.L.M. 368.
306 993 U.N.T.S. 3,6 I.L.M. 360.
307 I.L.O. Convention 169 Concerning Indigenous and Tribal Peoples in Independent Countries (1989).
308 United Nations Human Rights Commission, Draft Declaration on the Rights of Indigenous Peoples, E/CN.4/SUB.2/1994/2/Add.1 (1994).
309 Approved by Inter-American Commission on Human Rights on February 26, 1997, 1333rd session, 95th regular session.
310 U.N. Draft Declaration Article 7.
311 Id. at Article 7 (b).

HEED 8/98

lands, air, waters, coastal seas, sea-ice, flora and fauna and other resources which they have traditionally owned or otherwise occupied or used."[312]

• The right "to require that States obtain their free and informed consent prior to the approval of any project affecting their lands, territories and other resources." [313]

• The requirement that "The states shall not undertake, support or favor any policy of artificial or enforced assimilation of indigenous peoples, [or] destruction of a culture . . . ."[314]

The principal violations arise out of the Slave Lake oil and gas field which Unocal has operated since 1981.[315] Slave Lake lies in the Lubicon Cree's traditional lands in what is now the province of Alberta, Canada. Although the government is aware of their claims, the Lubicon have not reached an accord with the Canadian government regarding rightful possession of their lands. Unocal described the on-going political struggle of the Lubicon around Slave Lake on its web page:

> The [Slave Shallow Gas] plant's nearest neighbors are a small group of Lubicon Indians living 12 miles from the site. Because of the plant's proximity to a proposed reserve area for the Lubicon by the Canadian government, *Unocal has become caught in the middle of the Lubicon land rights dispute* with provincial and federal authorities. This dispute considerably predates any Unocal involvement in the region. Despite numerous attempts by authorities to settle the dispute, the claim remains unresolved. In recent years, three groups of Lubicon have broken away, formed separate bands and negotiated their own settlement with the government. As a result, membership in the original band — those still living near the Slave field — is thought to be considerably smaller. Authorities have noted that this could affect any further settlement, since an Indian reserve's size and amount of compensation are calculated according to its population base.[316]

---

312 Id. at Article 26.
313 Id. at Article 30.
314 Proposed American Declaration, article V.2.
315 Available on the Unocal Internet site (February 1998) www.unocal.com/globalops/lubicon.htm
316 Id.

HEED 8/98

The Lubicon's perspective, and the United Nations', is radically different. The Lubicon made an agreement with the Canadian government for a reserve which has yet to be created. In 1985, the Lubicon tried to gain an injunction to prevent resource exploitation on their land and were denied by the Supreme Court of Canada.[317] In 1988, in recognition of the impact development was having on the Lubicon's way of life, the United Nations called on the Canadian government to take steps to ensure no further damage be done to Lubicon society.[318] Canada continued to open exploitation of Lubicon land to outside corporations and in 1990, the United Nations Human Rights Committee found Canada to be in violation of Article 27 of the International Covenant on Civil and Political Rights. The Committee stated that the Canadian courts could not provide an effective remedy to the Lubicon for their losses.[319] Article 27 reads:

> In those states in which ethnic, religious or linguistic minorities exist, persons belonging to such minorities shall not be denied the right, in community with the other members of their group, to enjoy their own culture, to profess and practice their own religion, or to use their own language.

In official comments on Article 27, the Committee has noted that "Positive measures of protection are, therefore, required not only against the acts of the State party itself . . . but also against the acts of other persons within the State party."[320]

Unocal, a private actor, may be held liable for violations of these norms under the standard same legal doctrines that make it liable for human rights violations in Afghanistan and Burma, discussed in ear-

---

317 Heida Diefenderfer, "Lubicon Cree Impoverished as Multi-Nationals and Government Colonize Northern Alberta," *News From Indian Country,* August 15, 1997.

318 In response, the Canadian government sold a timber concession on almost the entire 4,000 square mile area Lubicon territory to Daishowa, a Japanese-based forestry company. Ed Bianchi, The Lubicon Lake Cree, *Akwesasne Notes,* March 31, 1996.

319 United Nations Human Rights Committee, Communication No. 167/1984 Bernard Ominayak, Chief of the Lubicon Lake Band v. Canada, 45th Session, Supplement No. 40 (A45/40), Volume II, pages 1-30.

320 United Nations Human Rights Committee, Article 27: 8/4/94 General Comment 23.

lier Counts.[321] See also the Yanomami Indians case,[322] Miskito Indians case,[323] and Finland Herdsmen's case.[324]

Unocal, far from being "caught" in the middle of the Canadian government and the Lubicon Cree, was a pioneer in exploiting and degrading Lubicon lands. Throughout the 1980's and 1990's, Unocal operated the Slave Lake oil and gas field. The first roads into Lubicon territory were cleared to allow exploitation of the Slave Lake field. In 1988, oil wells were shut down when the Lubicon set up "passport control points" on roads entering the disputed lands; police tore down the blockades and arrested 27 protesters.[325] In the summer of 1994, in spite of the Lubicon's objections and the United Nations' findings, Unocal constructed a $10 million sour gas plant only a little more than a mile upwind from the boundary of the proposed reserve the Lubicon and the Canadian government had previously agreed upon. Unocal was well aware of the boundaries of the negotiated reserve. The plant, which smells like rotten eggs, has further scarred the land and driven off the wildlife which the Lubicon depend on for their subsistence and their way of life.[326] The Lubicon believe their traditional economy has been deliberately destroyed by the governments of Canada and Alberta as part of a legal strategy. Canadian courts have ruled that those asserting Aboriginal land rights have to be able to show that they continue to pursue a traditional way of life. A gradual cultural genocide is thus a way to undermine land claims. As mentioned, the U.N. has warned Canada that it is improperly allowing this threat to Lubicon survival to occur. In this context, Unocal is complicit as a joint participant with the Canadian government and others in accomplishing a gradual cultural genocide.

---

321 See footnotes 231-237 supra.
322 Inter-American Commission on Human Rights Resolution No. 12/85, case 7615 (Brazil).
323 Inter-American Commission on Human Rights Report on Miskito Indians of Nicaragua OAS/Ser. L/V/II. 62 doc.10.rev.3, Nov. 1978.
324 United Nations Human Rights Committee, No. 511/1992 Oct. 26, 1992.
325 Sam Fletcher, "Unocal Logs 2 Indonesia Discoveries; Horizontal Well In Gulf Doubles Output," *The Oil Daily,* May 23, 1995.
326 Jack Danylchuk, "Lubicon, Catholic Order Force Debate on Start-Up of Unocal Sour Gas Plant," *The Edmonton Journal,* March 26, 1995; "In an Exploited Forest, an Indian Tribe Canada Forgot," *The Orange County Register,* August 4, 1996.

These violations work a forfeiture of Unocal's corporate charter because the charter has been "unlawfully exercised,"[327] and "perverted,"[328] in "serious offen[se]" against "the statutes regulating corporations,"[329] including the Unfair Competition Act prohibiting "any unlawful, unfair or fraudulent business act or practice,"[330] including business practices in violation of international law.

Ethnic tribes in Burma.

The relevant paragraphs from Count Five, supra, describing Unocal's business enterprise to build a pipeline in Burma are incorporated here by reference as if fully set forth.

Pursuing profits in its pipeline enterprise, Unocal has, in effect, taken sides in a civil war in which tribal peoples (in the pipeline region, principally the Karen and Mon peoples) are resisting the military dictatorship of the central government and asserting their rights to cultural and political survival that are guaranteed by customary international law, the Universal Declaration of Human Rights,[331] the International Covenant on Civil and Political Rights,[332] the International Covenant on Economic, Social and Cultural Rights,[333] and the International Labor Organization Convention No. 169 Concerning Indigenous and Tribal Peoples in Independent Countries.[334] The pipeline project has encouraged and even required Unocal's military business partner to intensify its civil war against the tribal peoples in the region in violation of the rights of these peoples under international law.

Unocal is liable for these acts by its military business partner under traditional doctrines of conspiracy agency, and joint participation. Unocal is also directly liable for these acts under the common-law torts of negligence, negligent hiring and negligent supervision.[335]

Unocal knew or should have known and could have reasonably foreseen that its military partner would intensify its civil war against the tribal peoples of the pipeline region.

---

327 California Code of Civil Procedure § 803.
328 *Dashaway*, supra note 69.
329 California Corporations Code § 1801 (a) (1).
330 California Business & Professions Code § 17200.
331 G.A. Res. 217(III), U.N. Doc. A/810 (1948).
332 999 U.N.T.S. 171, 6 I.L.M. 368
333 993 U.N.T.S. 3, 6 I.L.M. 360
334 I.L.O. Convention 169 Concerning Indigenous and Tribal Peoples in Independent Countries (1989).
335 See notes 231-237 supra.

Burma has been at war for more than four decades. . . . [A Total executive] conceded, "we know there might be a problem. . . [o]bviously the government has told us that they will make the area safe.". . . SLORC has mobilized troops in an area far wider than the actual route of the pipeline to . . . bring the ethnic populations under control. In this way, the pipeline has effectively furthered SLORC's economic as well as military agendas in southern Burma, as the contract is being used to legitimize SLORC military activities throughout the entire Tenasserim region.[336]

Unocal, in planning its business activities, has been aware, like the rest of the international community, of SLORC's ongoing battles to control and exploit Burma's ethnic lands. As already discussed under Count Six, the forced relocation of Karen villages is linked directly to the Yadana project. This act of cultural genocide has been part and parcel of SLORC's campaign to suppress ethnic minorities who live in valuable lands.

Unocal's participation in MGTC allows SLORC to accomplish ethnic domination in the name of "infrastructure" building and community development. A booklet published by Total and distributed by Unocal describes the companies' $6 million program of schools, clinics, livestock, roads, water and electricity to gain the support of inhabitants and explains its motivation: "The Yadana gas development project is the first industrial project of its kind to have been carried out in this underdeveloped and isolated region. It could not help but arouse a certain level of apprehension among the local communities."[337] The community assistance program, besides working neatly with the need for military pacification, disrupts the traditional culture in ways that may or may not be welcomed by local inhabitants if they could act freely and independently. Some Karen high school students, writing an open letter to Unocal from a refugee camp in Thailand, were critical:

[Y]ou said that if you give your western values and culture to the people in Burma then it will be interesting and good for them. But personally, we think that our ethnic groups in Burma are not interested in your culture. They want to keep and develop their own culture and live in freedom and peace.

---

336 *Total Denial*, supra note 220 at 13.
337 Total, *The Yadana Gas Development Project* 30 (1997).

Your culture is a very big culture, and so we are afraid [for] our small culture. Our small culture could be lost easily, because of your big culture. So, although you may think you have found the way to save our people in Burma from oppression it is actually the way to encourage the SLORC to push us down.[338]

338 *Total Denial,* supra note 220, Appendix C.

HEED 8/98

Count 9. Usurpation of Political Power

On the basis of the information stated and footnoted below, petitioners believe there is strong reason for the Attorney General to find the following to be true:

Unocal has exceeded the provisions of its charter and "usurped" political power that it cannot, by its corporate nature, exercise, thereby forfeiting its charter under the meaning of Code of Civil Procedure §803, Corporations Code §1801 (a) (2), and *The People ex rel. Attorney-General v. The Dashaway Association*, 84 Cal. 114, 119 (1890). As Chief Justice Marshall wrote in the *Dartmouth* case:

> [T]his being [the private corporation] does not share in the civil government of the country, unless that be the purpose for which it was created. Its immortality no more confers on it political power, or a political character, than immortality would confer such power or character on a natural person.[339]

Nor may Unocal claim a First Amendment shield for its political actions, because those actions move beyond the pale of even the free-speech rights conferred upon corporations by the U.S. Supreme Court in *First National Bank v. Belotti*. There, the court made clear that its decision did not extend to the situation where "corporate advocacy threatened imminently to undermine democratic processes, thereby denigrating rather than serving First amendment interests. . . ."[340] Aggressively undermining democratic processes at home and abroad Unocal has been:

• Intervening in the military and political conflicts of foreign nations.

As detailed in Counts Three through Seven above, Unocal has openly interjected itself into the military and political conflicts in Burma and Afghanistan, taking sides in each instance with brutal human rights abusers, giving them legitimacy, defending them publicly, working with them, and concluding or negotiating for business deals that promise major financial support to shore up their military oppression.

---

339 *Trustees of Dartmouth College v. Woodward*, 17 U.S. (4 Wheat.) 518, 636 (1819).

340 435 U.S. 765, 789 (1978).

HEED 8/98

In the case of Burma, Unocal has acted in hostile opposition to the democratically elected government, led by the National League for Democracy and Daw Aung San Suu Kyi, thus working to subvert the Burmese people's right to self-determination. The National Council of the Union of Burma (NCUB), an umbrella group representing the 1990 election winners and ethnic groups has stated that "only the democratically-elected government can explore, produce and sell the state's natural resources . . . . The NCUB has on previous occasions stated its request to the foreign companies not to invest in Burma until and unless the democratic government is allowed to fulfill its obligations endorsed by the Burmese people."[341] The National Coalition of Government of the Union of Burma, composed of elected officials, has declared:

> It is [our] duty to remind these companies that they are dealing with an illegal regime and represents no one but a small group of military personnel in Burma. The military regime has no mandate from the people to exploit or sell off the country's natural resources. Hence, any agreement undertaken with an illegal regime will not be honoured by the Burmese People.[342]

When Aung San Suu Kyi was released from six years of house arrest in 1995 to a chorus of international approval, Unocal remained silent, refusing even to comment on how the release might affect the company's investments.[343]

In the case of Afghanistan, Unocal is courting a militia faction that is not even a recognized government, flying the Taliban faction's "ministers" to Texas for negotiations, and in turn flying Unocal officers to Afghanistan, while the Afghanistan seat in the United Nations is occupied by the government which the Taliban ousted from the capital. Both U.S. Secretary of State Albright and first lady Hilary Clinton have condemned the Taliban's treatment of women. In a speech at a refugees camp in Pakistan, Secretary Albright criticized the treatment as "despicable."[344] But "Unocal . . . has pressed ahead . . . . The Taliban

---

341 *Total Denial*, supra note 220 at iii.
342 Quoted in *Total Denia* , supra note 220 at 6.
343 *Total Denial* , supra note 220 at 6.
344 Dan Morgan and David B. Ottaway, "Women's Fury Toward Taliban Stalls Pipeline," *Washington Post*, June 11, 1998 at A-1.

HEED 8/98

stands to collect $50 million to $100 million a year in transit fees if the pipeline is built . . . ."[345]

Behaving like a nation-state that chooses to recognize military forces as governments and pushes economic and political policy on foreign regimes, Unocal has decided to become a global economic and political force unto itself. The company acknowledges that "[a]s a global energy corporation, Unocal is a key player in the economies of many countries around the world -- particularly in southeast Asia."[346] Unocal boasts that "[w]e've . . .been a reliable, long-term partner with state-owned and private co-venturers in Thailand, Indonesia, the Philippines, and, more recently, in Myanmar,"[347] never mentioning that during much of Unocal's reliable partnership each of these countries has severely violated human rights. In pursuit of economic hegemony among nations suffering civil unrest, Unocal inevitably has turned itself into a political force.

• Subverting U.S. foreign policy.

The President and the Congress of the United States have opted for economic and political sanctions rather than "constructive engagement" as the appropriate foreign policy stance with Burma's totalitarian regime. Not Unocal. Unocal has decided constructive engagement is the desirable policy and works to thwart U.S. foreign policy with all the means at its disposal.

The U.S. has imposed sanctions against companies that do business in Burma. Under 1990 legislation, direct financial assistance and much international lending and aid were blocked.[348]

Unocal was unhappy with the policy. In 1996, Unocal President John Imle complained to Congress that

> the U.S. has not implemented a policy that even remotely resembles constructive engagement. If we continue traveling down the path of unilateral sanctions, we will be unable to lead by example not only in Myanmar but throughout the

---

345 Id.
346 "Another side to economic development," Unocal Internet site at www.unocal.com/pep/pepintro.htm.
347 "Developing Economies (Southeast and Central Asia)," Unocal Internet site at www.unocal.com/pep/pepasia.htm.
348 Customs and Trade Act of 1990, Pub.L. No. 101-383, sec. 138, 104 Stat. 629, 653 (August 20, 1990).

region. We will diminish our ability to influence construc-
tively the future of Southeast Asia and cede the opportunity to participate in the formative stages of Myanmar's
development [read: to profit from the dictatorship's infrastructure projects?].[349]

Congress rejected Imle's advice. In 1997, Congress imposed fur-
ther restrictions on bilateral assistance and authorized the President to
"prohibit United States persons from new investment in Burma, if the
President determines and certifies to Congress that the government of
Burma has physically harmed, rearrested for political acts, or exiled
Daw Aung San Suu Kyi or has committed large-scale repression of or
violence against the democratic opposition."[350] The President issued
Executive Order 13047 on May 20, 1997 implementing the sanctions.[351]
Although the sanctions apply only to new investment and therefore do not immediately affect Unocal's Burma pipeline, Unocal continues to fight U.S. foreign policy, It complains on its web site that
"some political groups opposed to Myanmar's current government
criticize U.S. investment in this country and call for economic sanctions to re-isolate this developing nation."[352] But it goes beyond this
free speech expression of its position. It spends $2 million a year on
"government relations, public communication and legal costs" related
to Burma.[353] Among other efforts, it deploys diplomats as if it were the
State Department itself. Unocal helped fund an organization that spon-
sored a trip to Burma in October, 1997, by Morton I. Abramowitz,
Richard L. Armitage and Michael H. Armacost.[354] Abramowitz was
ambassador to Thailand from 1978 to 1983 and Turkey from 1989 to
1991 and president of the Carnegie Endowment for Peace from 1991
to 1997. Armacost was ambassador to the Philippines from 1982 to

---

349 "Constructive Engagement In Myanmar," Testimony submitted to the U.S.
    Senate Banking Committee on S. 1511, May 22, 1996, by John Imle,
    President of Unocal Corporation.
350 Section 570 of The Foreign Operations, Export Financing, and Related
    Programs Appropriations Act, Pub. L. 104-208, Policy Towards Burma
    (Cohen-Feinstein Amendment, 1997), subsection 113 (b).
351 62 Fed. Reg. 28301 (May 22, 1997).
352 Unocal Internet site at www.unocal.com/myanmar/index.htm.
353 Unocal, "Proxy Statement for the 1998 Annual Meeting of Stockhold-
    ers," at 29 (April 20, 1998).
354 R. Jeffrey Smith, "Burma's Image Problem Is a Moneymaker for U.S.
    Lobbyists," *The Washington Post*, February 24, 1998 at A-19.

1984 and Japan from 1988 to 1993. Armitage was assistant secretary of defense in the mid-1980s. From these privatized high-ranking diplomats, Unocal got an opinion it liked: the team came back and recommended to the Clinton Administration that it eventually reconsider the sanctions policy.[355]

Unocal's business partner with a 15% interest in the pipeline project, the SLORC-owned Myanmar Oil and Gas enterprise (MOGE), is "the main channel for laundering the revenues of heroin produced and exported under the control of the Burmese army," according to a drug research group.[356] The group noted that despite the fact that MOGE "has no assets besides the limited installments of its foreign partners and makes no profit, and that the Burmese state never had the capacity to allocate any currency credit to MOGE, the Singapore bank accounts of this company have seen the transfer of hundreds of millions of US dollars.," more than $60 million of it "originating from Burma's most renowned drug lord, Khun Sa. 'Drug money is irrigating every economic activity in Burma,' Casanier [of Geopolitical Drug Watch] says, 'and big foreign partners are also seen by the SLORC as big shields for money laundering.'"[357]

The opium trade has boomed since SLORC took power in 1988. The U.S. government believes that the Burma economy is "awash in laundered drug money and that its military rulers have encouraged those who trade in drugs to invest in its development projects," according to the *New York Times*.[358] "'Drug traffickers who once spent their days leading mule trains down jungle paths are now leading lights in Burma's new market economy and leading figures in its new political order,' Secretary of State Madeline K. Albright told the Association of Southeast Asian Nations . . . last July."[359] The U.S. State De-

---

355 Id.
356 Dennis Bernstein & Leslie Kean, "People of the Opiate: Burma's Dictatorship of Drugs," *The Nation* (N.Y.), December 16, 1996, quoting Geopolitical Drug Watch, a Paris-based non-governmental organization that researches drug trafficking and issues an annual report based on information from 100 legal, academic, media and non-governmental organization correspondents around the world.
357 Id.
358 Christopher S. Wren, "Road to Riches Starts In The Golden Triangle," *New York Times*, May 11, 1998 at A-8.
359 Id.

partment estimates that 60 percent of the heroin seized in the United States is now coming from Burma, while our Embassy in Rangoon released a "Country Commercial Guide" in 1996 stating that at least 50 percent of Burma's economy is extralegal. "Exports of opiates alone appear to be worth about as much as all legal exports," the report says. "Barriers between the opiates sector and the legal economy appear to have weakened in recent years. . . ." [360]

In Afghanistan, too, Unocal is entwining itself with the drug traffickers. According to the U.S. State Department, "Afghanistan has become the second largest opium producer in the world."[361] The Taliban claim to forbid drug use but they control the opium growing lands and collect a tax from opium farmers.[362]

In 1997, a Unocal shareholder and retired worker in the Oil, Chemical and Atomic Workers International Union succeeded in putting a shareholder's resolution in the company's annual proxy statement asking the board of directors to research and report on the allegations about MOGE's drug connections as well as on the extent to which company officials have been aware of any facts supporting the allegations.

The company had strenuously tried to block the resolution from the proxy statement. Among other things, it argued that the allegations were "unrelated to Unocal's business operations in Myanmar," and that the investigation requested "would be illegal under Section 3(1) of the Myanmar Official Secrets Act [which] makes it illegal for any person, for purposes prejudicial to the safety or interests of the State, to obtain, publish or communicate to any other person any information which might directly or indirectly be useful to an enemy."[363] It asked the Securities and Exchange Commission to issue a letter promising the regulatory agency would take no action against the company if the company excluded the shareholder proposal from the proxy statement. The SEC refused to issue a no-action letter, saying it was "un-

---

360 Bernstein & Kean, supra note 356.

361 U.S. Department of State, *Afghanistan Country Report on Human Rights Practices for 1996* (January 30, 1997).

362 National Organization for Women, *The Day The Music Died: Women and Girls in Afghanistan*, Internet site at www.now.org/us-search/foundation.

363 Unocal Office of Chief Counsel, Letter to Securities and Exchange Commission Re: Stockholder Proposal of Wilborn Braughton, January 30, 1997.

able to concur" with Unocal's objections.[364] The resolution appeared in the proxy statement in 1997 and 1998, but attracted less than 6 percent of the voting stock each year, so the company is not investigating the alleged drug links.

Unocal's highly unorthodox efforts to counter our government's isolation of Burma, as well as its efforts to suppress information about its business partner's alleged laundering of drug money, are attempts to thwart U.S. foreign policy through the exercise of raw corporate power. This is "corporate advocacy threaten[ing] imminently to undermine democratic processes, thereby denigrating rather than serving First Amendment interests...."[365] And surely it is the duty of the Attorney General of California to put a stop to it, by recalling that California did not authorize Unocal to become a political actor, nor in the words of Chief Justice Marshall to "share in the civil government of the country."[366]

---

364 Securities and Exchange Commission, Response of the Office of Chief Counsel, Division of Corporate Finance, March 5,1997, Re: Unocal Corporation Incoming Letter Dated January 30, 1997.
365 435 U.S. 765,789 (1978)
366 *Trustees of Dartmouth College v. Woodward*, 17 U.S. (4 Wheat.) 518, 636 (1819).

HEED 8/98

Count 10. Deception of the Courts,
Shareholders and the Public

On the basis of the information stated and footnoted below, petitioners believe there is strong reason for the Attorney General to find the following to be true:

Despite public relations materials that gush with pieties about Unocal's "honesty," "integrity," "trust," "principles," "good neighbor" policies, "code of conduct," etc., the corporation has exhibited a pattern of deceiving the courts, its shareholders and the public about its activities, in violation of the Unfair Competition Act which proscribes any "unfair or fraudulent business practice."[367] These violations alone are sufficient grounds for the Attorney General to initiate charter revocation.

Pieties.

From Unocal's web page:[368] "Our vision: To improve the lives of people wherever we work. Be a good neighbor, actively involved in our communities." "Our values: Honesty--Open and honest with our partners and customers. . . . Integrity--Following the highest ethical standards. Following the letter and spirit of the law. Doing what we say we'll do. . . . Trust--Maintaining our reputation for reliability and integrity in our performance and our business practices. Treating others with respect and good will." "Code of Conduct for Doing Business Internationally: Meet the highest ethical standards in all of our business activities. . . .Treat everyone fairly and with respect. . . . Offer equal employment opportunity for all host country nationals, regardless of race, ethnic group or sex. . . .Protect the environment. . . .Communicate openly and honestly." "Environmental Principles: . . . .To develop and produce products that can be manufactured, transported and used safely. . . . To operate our plants and facilities in a manner that protects the health, environment and safety of our employees and the public."

These statements weave a web of deceit. Businesses, of course,

---

367 California Business and Professions Code § 17200. "[A]n 'unfair' business practice occurs when it offends an established public policy or when the practice is immoral, unethical, oppressive, unscrupulous or substantially injurious to consumers." *The People v. Casa Blanca Convalescent Homes*, 159 Cal. App. 3d 509, 530 (1984).

HEED 8/98

are permitted to engage in a certain amount of illusory "puffing" to sell products because consumers are not expected to take the puffing at face value. But the statements quoted are not product sales pitches. They are commitments by the Board of Directors on fundamental policy issues. Among the many illustrations that reveal those commitments to be a deception are the following salient ones:

Deception of the courts.

In 1996, a federal district judge found that a Unocal paralegal *altered data, withheld information* and gave *false responses* in verified court documents, "with either the tacit or overt approval of her superiors," i.e., Unocal in-house corporate counsel.[369] The suit was brought by a widow against Unocal for the manufacture of a solvent containing benzene which allegedly led to the leukemia death of her husband. The court specifically said it "finds, by clear and convincing evidence, the shifting and sometimes inconsistent excuses, evasions, and explanations offered by Unocal to be neither credible nor persuasive." [370] The court invited plaintiff's attorneys to propose referral of the matter to the Bar officials with disciplinary authority over the Unocal attorneys, holding:

> The real culprit is not some low-level paralegal who has taken a course on how to be a legal assistant. That paralegal works in a general counsel's office employing approximately 40 attorneys. She is supervised by attorneys, and those line attorneys are presumably supervised by the general counsel.[371]

Indignant, the judge admonished Unocal:

> Discovery is not just a game where all that counts is the ultimate score no matter how unethically the players behaved.[372]

---

368 www.unocal.com.

369 *Richardson v. Union Oil Company of California*, 167 F.R.D. 1 , 3 (1996), modified in part in 170 F.R.D. 333 (1996).

370 Id. at 4. Unfortunately, plaintiff=s counsel, satisfied with the procedural sanctions imposed at trial, did not pursue the judge=s suggestion that the matter be referred to the disciplinary authorities of the Bar.

371 Id. at 6.

372 Id. at 5.

The judge directly put the blame on the top lawyers:

> "[N]or . . . does the Court believe that this legal assistant altered documents by "mistake." Moreover, the fact that she was "chastised" — not fired outright for a grave infraction, not demoted, not put on probation, not even given a written reprimand in her personnel folder [court's footnote: In fact, she was given at least one raise . . . .] — speaks louder than any post-hoc explanation in a legal brief about the attitude of her superiors toward her flagrant misconduct.[373]

The general counsel of Unocal, the top superior of the paralegal, is Dennis P. R. Codon, a man who views moral conduct as one of his specialties: "I differ from some general counsel in that I enjoy outside activities like speaking. . . . My expertise is in ethics and in corporate governance, and that's what my speeches are about . . . . I see myself as the conscience of the company."[374]

Deception of shareholders.

• As detailed in Count Four above, Unocal has flatly maintained to its investors as well as the public that it is not doing business with any party in Afghanistan, while the press reports extensive business dealings with the anti-woman, anti-homosexual Taliban militia. Moreover, it is a fact that a contract exists with the University of Nebraska to train pipeline workers in Taliban territory. After being grilled at the annual shareholders' meeting on the question, the company posted a new, contradictory, but still deceptively worded explanation as its web page.[375]

• As detailed in a portion of Count Nine above describing the alleged drug trafficking link with Unocal's business partner MOGE in Burma, Unocal attempted to squelch a shareholder's proposal on the matter from appearing in the annual proxy statement, making an array of frivolous arguments to deprive shareholders of information necessary to make informed decisions. The arguments were uniformly rejected by the Securities and Exchange Commission.

---

373 Id. at 4.
374 "Corporate Brief, In-House Counsel," *The National Law Journal*, November 10, 1997 at 3.
375 See note 195 supra and accompanying text.

HEED 8/98

Deception of the public.

• As detailed in Count Five above, after years of stoutly denying that any forced labor had been used in connection with the Burma pipeline project, Unocal President John Imle admitted in a sworn deposition in the *John Doe I* litigation that "some porters were conscripted."[376]

• As detailed in Count Three above, Unocal characterizes its contract with the University of Nebraska for training "for both men and women" in Afghanistan as "humanitarian support" related to the corporation's "core values." In fact, the contract calls for training to meet "the manpower requirements of the proposed Unocal pipeline projects," and in fact only men have been trained, no women.

• The company has submitted to the U.S. Department of Labor, and posted on its web page, a *Humanitarian Report: Yadana Project* by Justice K. M. Aubhan and Reverend R. W. Timm.[377] "The significance of the Report," declares Unocal, "cannot be overstated. It provides objective evidence that Unocal and the Yadana pipeline have no involvement in human right violations...Funded by humanitarian organizations, two international human rights experts spent five days in Burma during January 1998 and visited villages along the pipeline route. There was no army presence during any interview."[378] The Report's cover letter from its authors states, "There was never any army or government presence...."[379]

In fact, the Report was "prepared in response to a Unocal representative,"[380] and Unocal paid the authors' airfare, hotel and meal expenses.[381] Moreover, the translator for the team was an employee of MOGE,[382] the SLORC-owned government agency that is Unocal's business partner, so there was government presence the entire time. Unocal's attempts to hide the facts of payment and government presence have resulted in a report with zero credibility.

• Unocal is one of a number of oil companies that are alleged to

---

376 See note 256 supra and accompanying text.
377 www.unocal.com/myanmar/timm2.htm.
378 www.unocal.com/myanmar/labor.htm.
379 www.unocal.com/myanmar/timm.htm.
380 Id.
381 Investor Responsibility Research Center, 1998 Company Report C E and E: 2, Unocal (May 11, 1998).
382 www.unocal.com/myanmar/timm2.htm.

1
2
3
4
5
6
7
8
9
10
11
12
13
14
15
16
17
18
19
20
21
22
23
24
25
26
27
28

have defrauded the public, including Indian tribes, out of hundreds of millions of dollars by underpaying the oil royalties due from leases on public lands. The state of California and the City of Long Beach first sued Unocal and other oil companies in 1973 and settled for $345 million in 1991. Then, the federal government began to investigate and announced it would attempt to collect $440 million for California leases alone, and more nationwide. One hundred percent of these oil and gas royalties in California go to the public schools, so it is really schoolchildren that Unocal and its oil industry peers are cheating. The U.S. Justice Department and other plaintiffs currently have massive litigation pending that attorneys estimate could settle for $2 billion to $5 billion because of the possibility of penalties and treble damages.[383] If Unocal's liability is borne out, this will be yet another example of the duplicity of the oil company in holding itself out to the public as a good corporate citizen. Examples of deceptive behavior given above are actionable violations of *Business and Professions Code* § 17200.

383 Representative George Miller, "Underpayment a Fueling at $2 Billion Taxpayers Scam," *Roll Call,* June 8, 1998.

HEED 8/98

RELIEF REQUESTED

This petition presents extensive, carefully documented evidence that Unocal is a dangerous scofflaw corporation with a trail of egregious harms stretching from its home in California to the other side of the globe. Much of the evidence, all alleged on information and belief, seems indisputable, some warrants further investigation. It is not the function of a petition of this nature to prove the case. The function under *California Code of Civil Procedure §803* is to provide the attorney general with well-marshaled evidence, specifying all sources so they are available for official evaluation, that there is "reason to believe" that the corporation is acting contrary to its charter and in violation of the laws of California. It is submitted on the face of this appalling record that if the attorney general of California is a reasonable person he cannot deny that the petition meets that threshold of providing such "reason to believe."

It is respectfully requested that the attorney general now fulfill his legal duty by bringing a judicial action under §803 initiating proceedings to dissolve Union Oil Company of California and to appoint a receiver and preserve company assets pending dissolution. We also request that the Attorney General ask the court to exercise its authority under *Corporations Code* § 1804 in winding up the company to "make such orders and decrees and issue such injunctions in the case as justice and equity require," in order to fully protect jobs, workers, stockholders, unions, communities, the environment, suppliers, customers, governmental entities, and the public interest.

HEED 8/98

1

2

3

4

5

6

7

8

9

10

11

12

13

14

15

16

17

18

19

20

21

22

23

24

25

26

27

28

Respectfully submitted,

The National Lawyers Guild
International Law Project for
Human, Economic and Environmental Defense (HEED)

By: _____
     Robert W. Benson
     Attorney and Professor of Law

_____
Michelle Sypert
Attorney

_____
Cynthia Anderson-Barker
Attorney, Working People Law Center

Date:_____

HEED 8/98

LATE ADDENDUM ON AFGHANISTAN

Counts Three, Four, Nine and Ten of the Petition discuss Unocal's activities related to the Taliban militia of Afghanistan. Those discussions need to be modified to reflect these late developments as the petition is about to be completed.

In late August, 1998 the United States launched a military attack on what it called suspected international terrorist camps in areas of Afghanistan under Taliban control. On August 21, 1998, Unocal posted a new statement on its web page in which it made several relevant points.

The company said, in part: "As a result of sharply deteriorating political conditions in the region, Unocal, which serves as the development manager for the Central Asia Gas (CentGas) pipeline consortium, has suspended all activities involving the proposed pipeline project in Afghanistan." Further, it stated: "Unocal will only participate in construction of the proposed Central Asia Gas Pipeline when and if Afghanistan achieves the peace and stability necessary to obtain financing from international lending agencies for this project and an established government is recognized by the United Nations and the United States."

And the company for the first time addressed the issue of women: "Unocal recognizes the legitimate concerns regarding the treatment of women in Afghanistan." It then went on to affirm that its funding of the University of Nebraska program is "consistent with our core values and business principles," is "skills training" but is *not* "designed to provide pipeline construction skills training. These programs [i.e., the Nebraska program and a CARE program] . . . include basic job skills training and education for both men and women, and elementary education for boys and girls."

Petitioners note:

1. Unocal has merely "suspended," not ended, its involvement in Afghanistan.

2. Unocal has conditioned its pipeline participation on stability, international lending agency support, and U.N. and U.S. recognition of a government. It has not conditioned its pipeline participation on restoration of human rights for women and homosexuals. Referring to

HEED 8/98

1   the Taliban's treatment of women, The New York Times editorialized
2   on August 15, 1998 that Unocal and other oil and gas companies should
    withhold their rewards "until the Taliban end their cruel policies."
3   3. The company's assertion that the University of Nebraska pro-
4   gram is not for pipeline construction skills, and that it includes women,
    is directly at odds with petitioners' information cited in footnotes 198
5   - 201 of the petition.

6

7

8

9

10

11

12

13

14

15

16

17

18

19

20

21

22

23

24

25

26

27

28

HEED 8/98

APPENDIX
UNOCAL PETITIONERS LIST

Attorneys: HEED (NATIONAL LAWYERS GUILD INTERNA-TIONAL LAW PROJECT FOR HUMAN, ECONOMIC AND ENVIRONMENTAL DEFENSE), 8124 W. 3rd St. NLG Suite 201, Los Angeles, CA 90048, ph: 213-736-1094, fax: 213-380-3769, heed@igc.org, Internet www.heed.net

HEED is an arm of the National Lawyers Guild in Los Angeles dedicated to using international law to protect the fundamental rights of present and future generations of human beings and the biosphere.

ACTION RESOURCE CENTER, Box 2104 Venice, CA 90294, ph: 310-396-3254, fax: 310-392-9965, arcla@envirolink.org

The Action Resource Center's mission is to spearhead and support campaigns that protect the environment, human rights and social justice; and to provide training and coordination for grassroots organizing, education and non-violent direct action.

ALLIANCE FOR DEMOCRACY

Alliance for Democracy of USA, 681 Main Street, Waltham, MA 02451, ph: 781-894-1179, fax: 781-894-0279, RDugger123@aol.com

Alliance for Democracy of Austin, TX, 8507 Lewis Mt. Dr. Austin, TX 78737, ph: 512-288-3170, fax: 512-288-4426, GMD1152@aol.com

Alliance for Democracy of San Fernando Valley, CA, 10432 Amigo Ave. Northridge, CA 91326, ph: 818-360-3201, william.forthman@csun.edu

The Alliance for Democracy is a new national, populist organization committed to ending the corporate domination of our economy, politics, government, culture, media and environment, and of the world of nations; to systemic change to base our economic system on democratic values; and to building a new, independent people's movement at the local, national and global levels.

GLORIA ALLRED, individual, 6300 Wilshire #1500 LA, CA 90048, ph: 213-653-6530

Gloria Allred is an attorney in Los Angeles, California whose law practice emphasizes women's rights and civil rights. She also hosts her own radio talk show.

AMAZON WATCH, 20110 Rockport Way Malibu, CA 90265, ph: 310-456-1340, fax: 310-456-0388, asoltani@igc.org

Amazon Watch defends the Amazon rainforest by monitoring and deterring ecologically unsound mega-projects. Amazon Watch investigates and disseminates critical information on large-scale development schemes in the frontier regions of the Amazon and also supports traditional peoples in their efforts to influence development decisions that impact their environments and their way of life.

ASIAN/PACIFIC GAYS AND FRIENDS, 7985 Santa Monica Blvd. Suite 109 Box 443, West Hollywood, CA 90046-5112, ph: 323-980-7874, fax: 323-860-7369, jaballiv@aol.com

A/PGF is the oldest and largest organization supporting gay Americans who trace their descent from the countries of Asia and the Pacific Islands. A/PGF strives to enhance self identity, pride and personal growth, while taking a leadership role in relevant political and social issues.

BURMA FORUM LOS ANGELES, 2118 Wilshire Blvd. #383 Santa Monica, CA 90403, ph: 310-399-0703, fax: 310-392-9965, bfla@freeburma.org

The Burma Forum, Los Angeles, was founded in 1990 by Burmese exiles and other supporters of democracy and human rights in Burma. The Burma Forum works closely with the Burmese government in exile and other members of the Free Burma Coalition to pressure corporations to withdraw from Burma until democracy in achieved.

DEMOCRACY UNLIMITED OF HUMBOLDT COUNTY, P.O. Box 27 Arcata, CA 95518, ph: 707-822-2242, fax: 707-822-3481, cienfuegos@igc.org

Democracy Unlimited of Humboldt County works to reclaim citizen authority over giant corporations. DUHC does grassroots organizing and education in California and SW Oregon, and acts as an information clearinghouse. It leads "First Steps in Dismantling Corporate Rule" workshops, and is currently running a ballot initiative on corporate rule in Arcata, CA.

EARTH ISLAND INSTITUTE, 300 Broadway Suite 28 San Francisco, CA 94133, ph: 415-788-3666, fax: 415-788-7324.

Earth Island Institute is a non-profit conservation organization head-quartered in San Francisco, California. It has approximately 50,000 members and doners in the United States and engages in efforts to conserve, protect and restore wildlife and natural habitats. Many Earth Island Institute staff and members are engaged in professional study and recreational use of marine ecosystems.

MICHAEL FEINSTEIN, P.O. Box 5631 Santa Monica, CA 90409, ph: 310-392-8450, fax: 310-392-8450, mfeinstein@pen.ci.santa-monica.ca.us

Michael Feinstein is an elected member of the Santa Monica (CA) City Council from the Green Party. He joins the petition as an individual citizen.

FEMINIST MAJORITY FOUNDATION, 8105 W. 3rd St. LA, CA 90048, ph: 213-651-0495, fax: 213-653-2689, femmaj@feminist.org

The Feminist Majority Foundation is a national women's rights organization dedicated to working for women's equality through public education, cutting-edge research, educational programs, and strategies to further women's equality and empowerment, to reduce violence toward women, to increase the health and economic well-being of women, and to eliminate discrimination of all kinds. The Feminist Majority has led a nationwide campaign to end Gender Apartheid in Afghanistan since the Taliban's takeover in 1996.

FREE BURMA COALITION, 225 N. Mills St. #210 Madison, WI 53706, ph: 608-250-4810, zni@students.wisc.edu

The Free Burma Coalition (FBC) is an umbrella group of organizations around the world working for freedom and democracy in Burma. Its mission is to build a grassroots movement inspired by and modeled after the anti-apartheid movement in South Africa. The Free Burma Coalition movement stands 100% behind the leadership of Daw Aung San Suu Kyi and the National League for Democracy (NLD), whom the people have recognized as the sole legitimate leaders of Burma.

FREE BURMA: NO PETRO-DOLLARS FOR SLORC, 1847 Berkeley Way Berkeley, CA 94703, ph: 415-695-1956, fax: 415-695-1956

The Free Burma: No Petro-Dollars for SLORC campaign, a project of the International Rivers Network, pressures US oil corporations invested in Burma to withdraw their operations from Burma until a true democratic government has been implemented. The campaign aims to ameliorate human rights abuses and environmental ruin that are perpetuated by multinational oil company projects.

GLOBAL EXCHANGE, 2017 Mission St. #303 San Francisco, CA 94110, ph: 415-255-7296, fax: 415-255-7498, medea@globalexchange.org

Global Exchange is a non-profit human rights organization. It educates the public about global issues through a variety of programs: Reality Tours take people to Cuba, Mexico, Brazil, Guatemala, South Africa, Ireland, India, Indonesia and many other locations; Fair Trade stores provide income for crafts producers in third world countries; the Public Education Program produces educational materials and organizes speaking tours of human rights activists from around the world.

RANDALL HAYES, 221 Pine St. San Francisco, CA 94104, ph: 415-398-4404, fax: 415-398-2732, rhayes@ran.org

Randall Hayes is President of Rainforest Action Network. He signs this petition as an individual particularly to affirm the standing of every individual on Earth to assert the right to be free from global environmental harm such as climate change.

NATIONAL LAWYERS GUILD

National Lawyers Guild of USA, 126 University Place 5th Floor NY, NY 10003, ph: 212-627-2656, fax: 212-627-2404, nlgno@nlg.org

National Lawyers Guild of Los Angeles, 8124 W. 3rd St. Suite 201 LA, CA 90048, ph: 213-653-4510, fax: 213-653-3245, 74603.3556@compuserve.com

National Lawyers Guild of San Diego, 1850 5th Ave. San Diego, CA 92101, ph: 619-233-1313, fax: 619-232-7313, mikaspencer@labornet.org

National Lawyers Guild of San Francisco, 558 Capp St. San Francisco, CA 94110, ph: 415-285-1055, fax: 415-285-5066, nlgsf@igc.apc.org

National Lawyers Guild of Santa Clara Valley, 131 George St. Santa Jose, CA 95110, ph: 408-287-1916

The National Lawyers Guild is a nationwide bar association of progressive attorneys, law students, legal workers and jailhouse lawyers. Founded in 1937 as the first bar association to prohibit discrimination on racial, religious, gender or other grounds, its guiding principle is that human rights are more sacred that property interests.

NATIONAL ORGANIZATION FOR WOMEN

National Organization for Women, 1000 16th St NW #700 Washington DC 20036, ph: 202-331-0066, fax: 202-785-8576, now@now.org

National Organization for Women (CA), 926 J St. #820 Sacramento, CA 95814, ph: 914-442-3414, fax: 914-442-6942, canow@canow.org

NOW is the largest organization in the United States dedicated to women's equality and civil rights.

PROGRAM ON CORPORATIONS, LAW AND DEMOCRACY, P.O. Box 246 S. Yarmouth, MA 02664, ph: 508-487-3151, fax: 508-487-3151, people@poclad.org

The Program on Corporations, Law and Democracy instigates democratic conversations and actions that contest the authority of corporations to govern. Its work is to help organizers challenge the mass-producing and mass-marketing of culture and law by artificial entities called corporations. To help people contest the authority of corporations to govern.

PROJECT MAJE, 0104 SW Lane St. Portland, OR 97201, ph: 503-226-2189, fax: 503-226-2189, maje@hevanet.com

Project Maje is an independent information project on Burma, particularly human rights, environmental and narcotics issues. The Project, founded by Burmese activist Edith T. Mirante in 1986, has for over a decade, researched and released reports about Burma's frontier regions. Project Maje is dedicated to raising international awareness of the situation in Burma and supporting the campaign for corporate withdrawal from Burma.

PROJECT UNDERGROUND, 1847 Berkeley Way Berkeley, CA 94703, ph: 510-705-8982, fax: 510-705-8983, steve@moles.org

Project Underground is a human rights and environmental organization that supports communities threatened by the mining and oil industries.

RAINFOREST ACTION NETWORK, 221 Pine St. San Francisco, CA
94104, ph: 415-398-4404, fax: 415-398-2732, kellyq@ran.org

The Rainforest Action Network works to protect the world's rainforests
and their inhabitants through education, grassroots organizing and non-
violent direct action. Through its network of 150 Rainforest Action Groups
worldwide, RAN focuses both on "market" campaigns which directly impact destructive trans-national corporations and on support of traditional
forest peoples in maintaining their traditional culture while developing
local, community-based economies.

HARVEY ROSENFIELD, P.O. Box 1980, Santa Monica, CA 90406, ph:
310-392-0522, fax: 310-392-8874, harvey@consumerwatchdog.org

Harvey Rosenfield is a consumer advocate, attorney, and director of
the Foundation for Taxpayer and Consumer Rights in Santa Monica, CA.

SURFERS' ENVIRONMENTAL ALLIANCE, 341 Alta St. Santa Cruz,
CA 95060, ph: 831-471-1493, fax: 831-466-3354, dardley@aol.com

Surfers' Environmental Alliance is a grassroots organization of all vol-
unteers aggressively dedicated to improving our coastal environment and
public access to the coast. SEA is committed to taking on the hard issues
that make a difference, to taking on even the largest corporate polluters,
persevering and winning, for everyone.

TRANSNATIONAL RESOURCE AND ACTION CENTER, P.O. Box
29344, San Francisco, CA 94129, ph: 415-561-6567, fax: 415-561-6493,
trac@igc.org

Transnational Resource and Action Center works to build links for
human rights, environmental justice and corporate accountability. TRAC's
website, Corporate Watch www.corpwatch.org is an online magazine and
Internet resource center for activists, journalists, students, teachers and
the general public.

Cynthia Anderson-Barker, Working People's Law Center, Los Angeles (State Bar
175764)

Professor Robert Benson, Loyola Law School (State Bar #68521)

José Luis Fuentes, Working People's Law Center, Los Angeles (State Bar #192236)

James Minuto, Los Angeles (State Bar #106041)

Michelle Sypert (State Bar #181148)

For The International Law Project for Human, Economic & Environmental Defense (HEED),

National Lawyers Guild, 8124 W. 3rd St., Suite 201, Los Angeles, CA 90048,
Tel. 213/736-

1094. Fax: 213/380-3769. E-mail: heed@igc.org. Internet: www.heed.net

---

LEGAL SUPPLEMENT
TO COMPLAINT LODGED WITH
THE ATTORNEY GENERAL OF CALIFORNIA

TO REVOKE THE CORPORATE CHARTER OF
THE UNION OIL COMPANY OF CALIFORNIA
(UNOCAL)

By Petitioners

- Action Resource Center
- Alliance for Democracy of U.S.A.
- Alliance for Democracy of Austin, TX
- Alliance for Democracy of San Fernando Valley, CA
- Gloria Allred, individual
- Amazon Watch
- Asian/Pacific Gays and Friends
- Burma Forum Los Angeles
- Democracy Unlimited of Humboldt County, CA
- Earth Island Institute
- Michael Feinstein, City Council Member, Santa Monica, CA, individual
- Feminist Majority Foundation
- Free Burma Coalition
- Free Burma — No Petro Dollars for SLORC
- Global Exchange
- Randall Hayes, individual
- National Lawyers Guild USA
- National Lawyers Guild, of Los Angeles, San Diego, Santa Clara Valley and San Francisco
- National Organization for Women
- National Organization for Women California
- Program on Corporations, Law & Democracy (POCLAD)
- Project Maje
- Project Underground
- Rainforest Action Network
- Harvey Rosenfield, individual
- Surfers' Environmental Alliance
- Transnational Resource and Action Center

APRIL 19, 1999

On September 10, 1998, Petitioners filed a Complaint with California Attorney General Dan Lungren requesting that he initiate judicial proceedings to revoke Unocal's corporate charter under California Code of Civil Procedure §803 and California Corporations Code §1801. Attorney General Lungren declined the request without analysis or explanation. Petitioners now refile the Complaint with California Attorney General Bill Lockyer, together with this Legal Supplement containing information that has come to light since September.

1. UNOCAL'S ATTACK ON THE ENVIRONMENT CONTINUES UNABATED:

Count 1. (pp. 42 et seq.) of the Complaint presents evidence of Unocal's disdain for the environment over several decades. The fundamental problem is that Unocal has never fully invested financially or ethically in the idea of accident prevention. Unlike the airline industry, for example, where the concept of safety is a fundamental part of the enterprise from the beginning of product design through operation, the oil industry prefers a "crash now, pay later" approach. This is financially smart for oil companies like Unocal because their toxic spills are often not caught, not caught for decades, or, when they are caught, not billed to them at the full environmental and social cost of the cleanup. Moreover, cleanup costs are often tax-deductible as a business expense, so taxpayers end up footing the bill. New evidence that Unocal continues to follow this policy includes:

• Unocal subsidiary Molycorp's mine at Mountain Pass **in San Bernardino County,** discussed at p.47 of the Complaint, has been listed in a new survey by the Environmental Protection Agency as California's **biggest polluter for 1991 and among the top 10 every year since.** "[B]reaks in 1996 spilled thousands of gallons of water containing lead and low-level radioactive materials onto public lands." "San Bernardino County Board of Supervisors," *The Press Enterprise* (Riverside, CA), October 28, 1998, at B-4. About 2,620 chemical, mining waste and other spills occurred at the Molycorp site between 1982 and 1998 according to the Lahontan Regional Water Quality Control Board, ranging from less than a gallon to 1.3 million gallons. "Molycorp Inc. Gets Order to Report Spills," *The Press Enterprise* (Riverside, CA), February 6, 1999 at B-3.

• Molycorp has raised the ire of citizens and the local government **in Canton Township, PA,** for its plan to build a **low-level radioactive waste storage facility in a residential area.** The company has been ordered by the Nuclear Regulatory Commission to clean up its site , but fierce opposition to the storage plan has arisen and local government officials declare that the plan violates local ordinances. Janice Crompton, "Protesters Gird for NRC Hearing on Molycorp Plan, " *Pittsburgh Post-Gazette*, April 11, 1999 at W-6.

- Molycorp is also the target of environmental complaints **in New Mexico**. In a long-running battle, Amigos Bravos in Taos and New Mexico Citizens for Clean Air and Water recently filed suit in U.S. District Court against the EPA claiming that Molycorp's waste-rock from a mine in Questa is one of the sources of **"an acidic soup of toxic metals that seeps into the Red River" and makes it run a "milky blue."** Plaintiffs want the EPA to stop the waste flow. Ian Hoffman, "Suit Seeks EPA Limits on Molycorp Wastes," *Albuquerque Journal,* March 27, 1999 at 2. "State water quality reports name the Red as one of the more heavily contaminated streams in New Mexico." *Id.*

- **In California**, Communities for a Better Environment (CBE) has sued 14 oil companies for **years of alleged benzene and toluene contamination in drinking water supplies** throughout the state. "CBE alleges that the contamination has been ongoing since at least 1994 through leaks in underground storage tanks, refineries, tank farms, marine terminals, gasoline piping and distribution and delivery systems." "Citizens Group Sues Oil Companies Under Prop. 65, Alleges Water Contamination," 7 *Mealey's Litigation Report: Emerging Toxic Torts* No. 23 (March 3, 1999). The suit seeks relief under Proposition 65 as well as Business & Professions Code Section 17200 prohibiting unfair business practices. Unocal is a defendant. It is proper to single out Unocal for charter revocation even though other oil companies are also accused of the same behavior because in Unocal's case this is simply one more allegation evidencing a much broader pattern and practice of violations warranting dissolution of the company.

- In the **Kenai National Wildlife Refuge in January, Unocal spilled some 2,520 gallons of oil from its 30-year old pipeline** running through the area, according to the Alaska Department of Environmental Conservation. "Workers Tackle Oil Spill in Alaska Wildlife Refuge," *Reuters* (January 11, 1999).

2. U.S. DEPARTMENT OF LABOR OFFICIALLY CONFIRMS EVIDENCE OF FORCED LABOR FOR UNOCAL'S BURMA PIPELINE.

In September, 1998 the United States Department of Labor, complying with a direction of the United States Congress, released the results of its official investigation of labor in Burma. U.S. Department of Labor, Bureau of International Labor Affairs, "Report on Labor Practices in Burma," (September, 1998), *www.dol.gov/dol/ilab/public/media/reports/ofr/burma/main.htm.*

The report directly contradicts Unocal's two key contentions in response to widespread charges that its pipeline in Burma benefited from forced labor (Petition, Count 5, pp. 74 et seq.). The company has dogmatically maintained that no forced labor was ever used for the pipeline project, and that the Ye-Tavoy railway line nearby (on which forced labor was used) is not related to the pipeline.

The U.S. Department of Labor report states:

• "The preponderance of available evidence warrants several conclusions about the use of forced labor on the pipeline project. For the early phases of the Yadana pipeline project, refugee **accounts of forced labor appear to be credible** in light of Embassy reporting about the pipeline and the Total [a Unocal business partner] documents to which it refers."

• "The urgency of building the **Ye-Tavoy railway**, which at one point involved 24 hour **construction by forced laborers** in 1996, [footnote] and the fact that the railway was scheduled to become operable at approximately the same time as the pipeline in 1998, suggest that the military placed a high priority on access to the **pipeline** provided by the **railway** and that **there is some relationship between these two projects**.[footnote]"

3. UNOCAL COMPLETELY WITHDRAWS FROM DEALINGS WITH THE TALIBAN IN AFGHANISTAN BUT ITS PREVIOUS DEALINGS STILL STAND AS GROUNDS FOR REVOKING ITS CHARTER

"Effective December 4, 1998, Unocal has withdrawn from the Central Asia Gas (CentGas) pipeline consortium for business reasons. Unocal no longer has any role in supporting the development or funding of this project.." "Unocal Statement On Withdrawal from the Proposed Central Asia Gas (CentGas) Pipeline Project," *www.unocal..com/uclnews/98news/centgas.htm..*

Petitioners' Counts 3 (Complicity in Crimes Against Humanity: Aiding Oppression of Women) and 4 (Complicity in Crimes against Humanity: Aiding Oppression of Homosexuals), pp. 60 et seq. and 71 et seq. of the Complaint are based upon Unocal's business dealings with the anti-woman, homophobic Taliban militia that controls most of Afghanistan.

Petitioners are pleased that the company has halted this offensive corporate behavior and gratified that the press credited our Petition to revoke Unocal's charter as one of the reasons the company decided to pull out of Afghanistan. "The decision was made under the pressure of low world oil prices, feminist groups that assailed Unocal's contacts with the Taliban, the fundamentalist Islamic movement that rules Afghanistan, and concern about the presence of the accused terrorist Osama bin Laden in the country. . . . The Feminist Majority Foundation, a Los Angeles group, petitioned the State of California to revoke Unocal's charter. . . ." Steven LeVine, "Unocal Quits Afghanistan Pipeline Project,"*The New York Times* , December 5, 1998 at C-2.

Counts 3 and 4 still stand, however, as grounds for revocation of Unocal's charter. A charter revocation is concerned neither with correcting company behavior, nor with penalizing it for past conduct. Revocation looks to the future, seeking to guarantee that corporations that are likely to act nefariously in the future are prevented from doing so by forfeiting their corporate existence. A company that for two years was willing to become complicit in crimes against women and homosexuals by supporting an extremist military regime that oppresses them, and then cites only "business reasons" when it drops its complicity, is a company that is not to be trusted in the future to act responsibility, legally, and in accord with the public policies of the State of California.

4. <u>COMPANY PERSISTS IN DECEPTION OF PUBLIC AND SHAREHOLDERS.</u>

Count 10 of the Petition, pp. 114 et seq., describes a pattern of deception which Unocal still seems unable to break. Since the Petition was filed Unocal:

• Has offered no explanation for why it publicly insisted it was not conducting or negotiating business with the Taliban when so many press reports were to the contrary (Petition pp.66-68).

• Has baldly repeated its claim that its program with the University of Nebraska field operation in Afghanistan was "humanitarian" and "skills training" that included "basic job skills training and education for both men and women, and elementary education for boys and girls." "Unocal Statement On Withdrawal from the Proposed Central Asia Gas (CentGas) Pipeline Project, *www.unocal..com/uclnews/98news/centgas.htm.*. In fact, the contract called for meeting the "manpower requirements of the proposed Unocal pipeline projects," the University program head was quoted in the press stating that the program was " 'to help the company' get the pipeline built," the Taliban prohibited the University from training women in the program, and no education for girls was undertaken in Taliban areas. See Petition, pp. 68-70.

• Has issued a scathing statement to U.S. Labor Secretary Alexis Herman calling the Department's September, 1998 "Report on Labor Practices in Burma," "baseless," founded on "insinuation and innuendo," "biased," "false," and "irresponsible." Unocal calls for "an investigation into the methods and procedures" used by the Department, including possible "conflicts of interest and misrepresentations by the consultant-activist who was hired" for the report. *www.unocal.com/myanmar/dolletr.htm.* This intemperate denunciation served to generate heat and smoke, allowing Unocal cover to slip away from the issue without ever offering a thoughtful, point by point rebuttal of the Department's evidence. In presenting its own evidence to the Department in advance of the September report, Unocal did not mention that it paid for the travel and lodging expenses of the authors of its "Humanitarian Report: Yadana Project" by Justice K.M. Aubhan and Reverend R.W. Timm. Nor has Unocal acknowledged the significance of the fact that the authors were accompanied by a translator who was a Burmese government employee. See Petition, p. 188.

• Has posted a "discussion paper" on its web site entitled "Human Rights and Unocal," which is filled with pious devotion to international human rights and even goes so far as to reprint the entire Universal Declaration of Human Rights and to set up an e-mail link for "feedback" and "discussion." This is a transparently disingenuous attempt to counter the poor public image that has resulted from the company's disregard of human rights. The approach seems lifted out of the manual of "strategic consultants" who have been advising corporations recently to blunt criticism of their operations by appearing to adopt the values of their critics and opening dialogues with them. The approach is that of a lightning rod: deflecting heat while allowing the company to carry on business as usual. Unocal's "discussion paper" deceives by drawing the reader into esoteric, theoretical conundrums of human rights law without ever addressing the very straightforward, concrete violations of human rights law alleged in our Counts 3-8, and in the two law suits pending in U.S. District Court Central District of California against Unocal for its activities in Burma, *John Doe I et al. v. Unocal Corp. et al.* (Case No. 96-6959) and *National Coalition Government of Burma et al. v. Unocal* (Case No 96-6112RAP). A company genuinely concerned for human rights would publicly confront, point by point, the facts and the legal bases for human rights liability that have been alleged against it.

5. OTHER UPDATES

• **Tobacco industry corporations dissolved in New York.** Page 26 of the Complaint, reporting that the Attorney General of New York State had moved to revoke the charters of two tobacco-industry related corporations, is updated as follows: Both the Council for Tobacco Research and the Tobacco Institute are now being dissolved. The industry agreed to dissolve them as part of the settlement of multi-state litigation by state attorneys general. The dissolution of the Council for Tobacco Research was accomplished when the industry agreed not to oppose the revocation action in New York. The judge hearing the New York Attorney General's charter revocation suit approved a plan for ending the Council's existence and donating its assets to the New York State University at Buffalo Health Sciences Center and the Roswell Park Cancer Center. Betsy Jelisavocic, "Plan to dissolve research group funded by industry gets judge's OK," *The Herald-Sun* (Durham, NC), October 25, 1998. The Tobacco Institute has closed its doors, but it is not yet clear how the actual dissolution will be accomplished. 12 *Mealey's Litigation Report: Tobacco*, No. 19 (February 4, 1999).

• **Table of Authorities.** Page ix, line 8 citing the Declaration on Torture, should also cite the Convention Against Torture and other Cruel, Inhumane or Degrading Treatment or Punishment (1465 U.N.T.S. 85) which the United States ratified on October 21, 1994.

Page ix, line 20 citing the International Covenant on Civil and Political Rights should note that the United States ratified this Covenant on June 8, 1992.

Respectfully submitted, April 19, 1999

Robert Benson, Attorney for
National Lawyers Guild, Los Angeles
The International Law Project for Human, Economic & Environmental Defense (HEED)

Appendix
Endorsers of Petition to
Revoke Unocal's Charter:

The petition was filed on September 10, 1998 by 30 individuals and organizations. Since then many others have endorsed, bringing the total coalition to nearly 150 and continuing to grow. In the approximate order received endorsers are:

1. Dan Hamburg, Green Party candidate for Governor of California.
2. Sara Amir, Green Party candidate for Lieutenant Governor of California.
3. Women's International League for Peace & Freedom, U.S. Section
4. Occidental, California Arts & Ecology Center
5. Green Party of Mendocino County, California
6. Alliance for Democracy of Birmingham, Alabama
7. Alliance for Democracy of Mid-Atlantic and District of Columbia
8. Alliance for Democracy of Delta County, Colorado
9. Global Response
10. Boulder Friends for a Democratic Burma
11. Amigos Bravos: Friends of the Wild Rivers, New Mexico
12. International Gay and Lesbian Human Rights Commission
    iglhrc@iglhrc.org
    IGLHRC's mission is to protect and advance the human rights of all people and communities subject to discrimination or abuse on the basis of sexual orientation, gender identity, or HIV status. Visit us on the web at http://www.iglhrc.org.
13. Professor Christine Littleton
    UCLA Law School
14. Professor Bryan Ford
    Santa Clara University School of Law
15. Professor Holly Maguigan
    NYU School of Law
16. Professor Chantal Thomas
    Fordham University School of Law

17. Professor Anthony Paul Farley
    Boston College Law School
18. Professor Sheryll Cashin
    Georgetown University Law Center
19. Professor Jane Dolkart
    Southern Methodist University School
20. Professor Katherine Sheehan
    Southwestern University School of Law
21. Professor Suzanne Jackson
    American University Washington College of Law
22. Professor Donna Coker
    University of Miami School of Law
23. Professor Patricia Leary
    Whittier Law School
24. Professor Nancy Ehrenreich
    University of Denver College of Law
25. Professor Robert Westley
    Tulane University School of Law
26. rofessor Terry Smith
    Fordham University School of Law
27. Professor Reynaldo Valencia
    St Mary's University of San Antonio School of Law
28. Professor Guadalupe Luna
    Northern Illinois University School of Law
29. Professor Norman Stein
    University of Alabama School of Law
30. Professor Darryl Wilson
    Stetson Law School
31. Professor David Oppenheimer
    Golden Gate University School of Law
32. Professor Elaine Anderson
    University of California, Hastings College of Law
33. Professor Deborah Maranville
    University of Washington School of Law
34. Professor David Casey
    Western State University School of Law
35. Professor Robert Gray
    Texas Wesleyan School of Law
36. Professor Cynthia Lee
    University of San Diego School of Law

37. Professor Theresa Glennon
    Temple University School of Law
38. Professor Majjorie Cohn
    Thomas Jefferson School of Law, San Diego
39. Professor Ruth
    University of Connecticut School of Law
40. Professor Paula Johnson
    Syracuse University College of Law
41. Professor Sylvia Law
    N.Y.U. Law School
42. Professor Annette Appell
    U.W.L.V. School of Law
43. Professor Robert Chang
    Loyola Law School
44. Professor Karen Czapanskiy
    University of Maryland School of Law
45. Professor Barbara Bezdek
    University of Maryland School of Law
46. Professor Sumi Cho
    De Paul University School of Law
47. Professor Desieree Kennedy
    University of Tennessee School of Law
48. Professor Catharine Wells
    University of Britsh Colombia
49. Professor Joan Howarth
    Golden Gate University School of Law
50. Professor Carol Chomsky
    University of Minnesota School of Law
51. Professor Amy Kastely
    St. Mary's University School of Law
52. Professor Lisa Ikemoto
    Loyola Law School
53. Professor Neil Gotanda
    Western State University School of Law
54. Professor Stephanie Wildman
    University of San Francisco School of Law
55. Professor Phoebe Haddon
    Temple University School of Law
56. Professor Fran Ansley
    University of Tennessee College of Law

57. Professor Karl Manheim
    Loyola Law School
58. Americans for Democratic Action in Los Angeles
59. Los Angeles City Council Member Jackie Goldberg
60. Green Party of Connecticut
61. 20/20 Vision of Central California
    www.2020vision.org
62. Alliance for Democracy, Santa Cruz, California
63. Pat Veesart, Director
    EcoSLO*
    1446 Morro St.
    San Luis Obispo, CA 93401
    805/544-1777
64. Green Party of San Luis Obispo County
    contact: Orval Osborne
    oosborne@igc.org
65. Joe Linton, Board Secretary
    Friends of the Los Angeles River*
    White House Place
    Los Angeles, CA 90004
    213/381-3570
66. Leland Stewart, Central Coordinator
    Unity-and-Diversity World Council*
    5521 Grosvenor Blvd.
    Los Angeles, CA 90066
    310/577-1968
67. Reverend Michael Mata
    Director, Urban Leadership Institute
    1010 S. Flower Su. 220
    Los Angeles, CA 90015
68. CRSP
    3551 White House Pl.
    Los Angeles, CA 90004
    213/738-1254
69. LA EcoVillage
    117 S. Bimini Pl.
    Los Angeles, CA 90004
    213/487-2305
70. Nancy Pearlman
    Ecology Center of Southern California

PO Box 351419
Los Angeles, CA 90035
310/559-9160

71. David Tokofsky
    Member Los Angeles City Board of Education
    450 N. Grand Ave.
    Los Angeles, CA 90640

72. Julia Russell
    Eco-Home Network*
    4344 Russell Ave.
    Los Angeles, CA 90027

73. Sheila Bernard
    Lincoln Place Tenants Association*
    Los Angeles, CA
    310/452-4956

74. Country Connections
    Catherine R. Leach, co-editor, co-publisher
    14431 Ventura Blvd. #407
    Sherman Oaks, CA 91423
    818/501-1896

75. Pure Foods Research Company
    Michael Moore, Trustee
    P.O. Box 156
    Lookout, CA 96054

76. Precise Nutritional Care
    Elizabeth Huntley, Ph.D.
    12342 Roscoe Blvd.
    Sun Valley, CA 91352
    818/767-5863

77. Arthur Kennedy, Boardmember
    Isla Vista Food Co-op*
    805/968-1401

78. Lynne Elizabeth, Editor
    New Village Journal
    2721 Stuart Street
    Berkeley, CA 94705 USA
    510/845-2481
    editor@newvillage.net
    a Publication of Architects\Designers\Planners for Social Responsibility

79. Bob Banner
    Publisher and Editor of HopeDance Magazine
    PO Box 15609
    San Luis Obispo, CA 93406
    805/ 544-9663
80. Renee Hill
    Peace & Justice Priest
    All Saints Episcopal Church*
    132 N. Euclid Ave.
    Pasadena, CA 91101
    626/583-2462
81. David Snyder, Executive Director
    San Francisco Bicycle Coalition*
    1095 Market St., Su. 215
    San Francisco, CA 94103
82. John Harrington, President & CEO
    Harrington Investment, Inc.
    an investment advisory firm
    1001 2nd St., Su. 325
    Napa, CA 94559
    800/788-0154
83. Janet Bridgers, President
    Domain Earth
    520 Washington Blvd. Su. 484
    Marina Del Rey, CA 90292
    310/204-0533
84. Labor/Community Strategy Center
    3780 Wilshire Blvd.   Su. 1200
    Los Angeles, CA 90010
    213/387-2800
85. One Stop Immigration & Education Center
    3600 Whittier Blvd.
    Los Angeles, CA 90023
    323/268-8472
86. Phildelphia II,
    1600 N. Oak St. #1412, Arlington, VA 22209-2757
    (703)516-4056, fax: (703)516-4057
    mike.gravel@cogroup.com
    Phildelphia II, 55 New Montgomery St. #225
    San Francisco CA 94105 (415)227-4880, fax: (415)227-4878

wfaofnca@wenet.net

Phildelphia II is a California nonprofit public benefit corporation that seeks to bring into being a process by which all citizens of the United States may participate in direct democracy via the mechanism of citizen's initiatives.

87.   One World
      1600 N. Oak St. #1412, Arlington VA 22209-2757
      (703)516-4056, fax: (703)516-4057
      mike.gravel@cogroup.com
      One World, 55 New Montgomery St. #225
      San Francisco CA 94105 (415)227-4880, fax: (415)227-4878
      wfaofnca@wenet.net
      One World is a California nonprofit public benefit education corporation that seeks to educate all people with respect to human governance at the world, national, and state levels.

88.   Reverend James Conn
      United Methodist Church*
      230 Pacific #108
      Santa Monica, CA 90405
      310/392-5757

89.   Mike Watanabe, Executive Director
      Asian American Drug Abuse Program, Inc.*
      5318 S. Crenshaw
      Los Angeles, CA 90043
      323/293-6284

90.   Environmental Defense Center
      906 Garden St.
      Santa Barbara, CA 93101
      805/963-1622

91.   Sylva Blackstone, Boardmember
      Theodore Payne Foundation*
      PO Box 93680
      Pasadena, CA 91109
      323/255-1983

92.   Hari Dillon, President
      Vanguard Public Foundation*
      383 Rhode Island St., Su. 301
      San Francisco, CA 94103
      415/487-2113

93.   Social and Environmental Entrepreneurs, Inc.

20110 Rockport Way
Malibu, CA 90265
310/456-3534

94. Michelle Mascarenhas, Director
Community Food Security Project*
Occidental College
323/259-2633
mm@oxy. edu

95. Mike Davis, Author
Ecology of Fear
amoctezuma@earthlink.net

96. Edward Weber
Chapter Chair, Yorkdale Elementary
North Area House of Reps, United Teachers of Los Angeles
1661 S. Oxford Ave.
Los Angeles, CA 90006

97. Dr. Gary Crane, Director
Ideal Communications
805 Allott Ave.
Van Nuys, CA 90412
818/780-4533

98. Southern Appalachian Biodiversity Project
PO Box 3141
Asheville NC 28802
828/258-2667

99. Images Asia
Chiang Mai, Thailand
a Thai / multicultural NGO
edesk@cm.ksc.co.th

100. Howard Clinebell, Professor Emeritus
School of Theology
Claremont, California
805-687-7777

101. California State Senator Tom Hayden

102. California State Assemblywoman Audie Bock

103. Greenpeace USA Climate Campaign
carwil.james@wdc.greenpeace.org
(202)319-2406

104. Ron Milam, Executive Director
Los Angeles Bicycle Coalition

rpm@labikecoalition.org
105. Social Concerns Committee
     Unitarian Church of Orange County Universalist
     Anaheim, CA
106. Kevin McKeown
     Santa Monica City Councilmember
     Santa Monica, CA (USA)
     310 393-3639 /-3609 FAX
     email: kevin@mckeown.net
     http://www.mckeown.net
107. The Institute for Economic Democracy
     San Luis Obispo, CA 93403-3254
     Phone/Fax (805) 786-0307
     jwsmith@slonet.org
     www.he.net/~jwsmith
108. Suza Francina
     Mayor Pro Tem
     Ojai City Council
     sfrancina@aol.com
109. Jamie Lee Evans
     Director of Teen Education
     San Francisco Women Against Rape*
     (415) 861-2024
110. Larry Robinson
     Councilmember
     Vice-Mayor Sebastopol
     Sonoma County
     lrob@pon.net
111. Colby C.Crotzer
     Morro Bay City Councilmember
     colby@fix.net
     (805)772-9253
     475 Arbutus Ave.
     Morro Bay, CA 93442
112. Rick Skillan
     Los Padres Chapter Chair
     Sierra Club*
     (805) 735-4190
113. The Social Justice Committee of the
     San Luis Obispo County Unitarian Universalist Fellowship (UUF-

SLO)
Contact: Orval Osborne
(805) 549-9791
oosborne@igc.org
114. Mayor Bob Ornelas
City of Arcata, CA
115. Julie Partansky,
Mayor, City of Davis
116. Epicenter Inc. of Boulder, Colorado.
Contact Jeff Milchen at epi@indra.com

*Asterisk indicates "for identification only." Endorsements are added to the end of the list roughly in the order received. To endorse, send an e-mail to: heed@igc.org.